TRAGIC WHISPERS

Secrets From The Heart Of
A Broken Palestinian American Women

BY

DEANA ELAINE

Book Writing Genie

TABLE OF CONTENTS

DEDICATION

To my mother, Rhoda Gay Salman, whose life traumas, strength, and spirit shaped me in ways I now understand.

You now, after so many years have given me

'Generational Healing,' which has come through the

"Matriarch of our family"

"The Lord has vindicated us: come, let us tell Zion what the Lord our God has done."

Jerimiah 51:10

ACKNOWLEDGMENT

To my husband, Anthony

You have honored me and stood by my side through the good, the bad and the ugly for over 16 years now. You have never refused to give up on me, always telling and showing me, I am worthy of love. You have been a father to my children in depths that I could not fathom. Thank you for your persistence and encouraging me to write my life story. I love you with all my heart.

To my brother, Max

My story would not be complete if it were not for the love and encouragement, sometimes harsh, but always in my best interest that you continually shower over me. Throughout all my years before my husband *Anthony*, you have been the only real man in my life to show love, compassion, and strength when I was at my lowest in my years of trauma.

I genuinely believe I could not have survived what comes over the next 60 years if you were not by my side, brother.

To my children, Jamal, Ellie, Nasser, Amira & Madison Rae

To whom you will come to know through out the forthcoming books…

You all were always there for me, encouraging me to tell my story. Enduring all my emotions, pain, and addiction, but most of all, giving me the love, encouragement, validation, and forgiveness a mother always longs for and needs from their children during their life journey, as each of you has given me.

To relatives and friends, you will come to know. Thank you for being there to encourage, pray, help, and love me for me. You all have been so powerful in your support of my book.

ABOUT THE AUTHOR

I was born into a world of opposites—my father, a proud man from Palestine, and my mother, a spirited woman from Kentucky. Their roots could not have been more different, and somehow, I found myself caught between them.

My life became a search—a search for the love of a father and the safety of a mother, a journey marked by marriages and separations, by new cities and motherhood, by addiction and painful lows, by therapy and slow healing.

I built a career with sheer grit just to be seen. I have been a licensed hairdresser for over 25 years, also worked at the 1999 Miss USA Pageant, grooming Miss New York every day until she took the crown.

The following year, I was there when Christina Aguilera performed and was asked to groom her for the pageant entertainment. I opened several salons, taught for brands such as Matrix and Sunglitz, and eventually got into medical aesthetics with Hanna Isul, creating my own line of hair care and makeup along the way.

Then, life took me to the kitchen. I started several pizza restaurants in Texas and later opened a Mediterranean-Italian restaurant and catering business in Phoenix. Those chapters came with their own lessons, bruises, and joys.

After years of trauma and addiction, of lying to myself and to others, I reached a breaking point, and by the grace of God, I found a way to start fresh.

Now, at 63, I have a life that is real, one I never thought I deserved. I have five incredible children and a husband of 16 years, and I am slowly mending the broken parts of my past. I can finally say I am whole.

"By the grace of GOD, I am what I am, and this grace towards me was not in vain."

— Corinthians 15:10

FOREWORD

Have you ever asked yourself if your parents kept you safe? If your life has been touched by trauma, family drama, dysfunction, addiction, or mental illness, then I invite you to journey with me. I am a Palestinian American woman who has lived through all of this—a life that I hope will resonate with many who know these struggles all too well.

Step into my story. Walk with me through events that will keep you on the edge of your seat, events so vivid you may question if they are even possible, yet they are, and they are happening all around us, even now, even here.

"A memory is what is left when something happens and does not completely unhappen."

— Edward de Bono

"Fear is the memory of pain. Addiction is the memory of pleasure. Freedom is beyond both."

— Deepak Chopra

Signs of Unhealed Childhood Trauma

Anxiety, depression, trouble forming relationships, emotional outbursts, low self-esteem, intrusive memories, trust issues, self-destructive behaviors, chronic stress, substance abuse, dissociation, sleep disturbances, physical symptoms, and boundary struggles.

— www.mentalhealthcenter.org

It often lingers in the stomach, abdomen, lower back, upper torso, chest, shoulders, and spine.

— *www.wcsap.org*

Children, especially those from 0-5, are most vulnerable to trauma, as their brains are still in critical stages of development.

— *www.lookthroughtheireyes.org*

"The Lord is close to the brokenhearted and saves those who are crushed in spirit."

— Psalm 34:18

PREFACE

If you are picking up this book, chances are you know a thing or two about life's ups and downs. Maybe You have faced challenging times, felt a bit lost, or wondered if things would ever truly fall into place. You are not alone—I have lived it, too.

My story starts with two wildly different worlds colliding. My father is a Palestinian with deep-rooted traditions and pride, and my mother is a spirited woman from Kentucky. Together, they brought their worlds into my life, setting me on a path filled with conflict, dreams, disappointment, and sometimes what I thought was love. Between family drama, cultural divides, and personal struggles, I spent years chasing what I thought was missing—unconditional love and a place where I could feel safe.

In these pages, I will share my journey. Not as a fairytale but as the real, raw story it is. It is a story filled with tough moments and hard-won lessons. I hope, as you read, you will find parts that resonate with your own life, parts that remind you of your strength and the resilience within you. Life has not been simple or easy, but through it all, I have found a type of peace I did not think was possible.

So, I invite you to walk alongside me through these memories. Maybe, together, we will find that even in the hardest chapters, there's hope, healing, and a chance to write a new ending.

Chapter One

EVERYONE HAS A STORY
THIS IS MY STORY

Born September 26, 1961, Deana Elaine Salman

In the quiet heart of *El-Bireh, Ramallah, Palestine*, the small two-room hut bore witness to a life that would one day stretch across the continents. It was May 21, 1929, and within these modest walls, a boy named *Fateeh Abdel Fatah Salman (Dar Toweel,* which means *"The Big House"*) was born to *Abdel Fatah & Fatimah Salman.* They lived in a two-room hut, with their four children raised mainly by my Sitee (grandmother), as my Seedo (grandfather) came to the United States to seek out his opportunities.

After years abroad, he returned to his hometown in the early 1950s, settling back into the same modest home. Despite only having a 5th-grade education, my father became an extraordinarily successful, influential businessman in the United States starting in his early 20s. *Yabbah* (father) arrived at *Ellis Island* on a boat and was then granted a temporary visa to explore the land of opportunity - America!! Now being called *Al Salman.*

With a visa for a period of time, his plan was to eventually return to his country, as his father did. He had one brother and two sisters, all younger than him. They all came to America at one time or another but eventually chose to return to Palestine, except for (Ummo) *Charlie*, my biological aunt *Nejah's* (Umptie), who was my father's baby sister's husband. I only name some of his family members, as some of my father's siblings are important due to being a huge part of my early years of life. His other siblings… I could care less about and will honestly say that I felt justified as I heard how each one passed a slow, miserable death. I still pray I can forgive them for their actions.

Beloved, do not be obsessed with taking revenge, but leave that to God's righteous justice. For the scripture, say: "Vengeance is mine, and I will repay, says the Lord."

NIV Romans 12:19-21

Umptie *Nejah* went back home to raise her children within their culture. Ummo *Charlie*, an entitled businessman, shuttled between the U.S. and Palestine, owning several businesses, including a bar named *The Paramount* in Toledo, Ohio. You will see how this last statement will come into play later in my journey of life.

My father was a hustler till the day he died. At age 20, he eventually made it to Gary, Indiana, where he sold replica Timex watches and just about anything else inside his trench coat, much like in the movies. He once told a story about being nailed by some *"Corner Cops"* while doing his hustle on the street corner. I can literally still hear his giggles when he would tell the story! I guess because he was so thin, he slipped out of the handcuffs, never to be seen on that street corner again!!

His hustle continued, eventually marrying Judith, and having two children, *Annie & Freddy*, in Gary, Indiana. *Judith's* arranged marriage for a mere $500 at age 16 reflected the ongoing practice of such marriages, even in America. My father later partnered with a man to own a bar in Gary, Indiana. The bar was in a rough neighborhood, as were many of his early ventures, but they all had one thing in common - the mighty greenback!!

However, the one thing that rocked his world was meeting and falling madly in love with a new barmaid, *Rhoda Gay Nickell,* my mother

Rhoda Gay Nickel was born August 14, 1936, in West Liberty, Morgan County, Kentucky, to *Alonzo & Dora Adams Nickell.* The *Nickell* family has a storied history, with *River Tom* being just one example of our far-reaching lineage.

Alonzo & Dora Adams Nickell

Tom Horn shot and killed a 14-year-old boy, Willie Nickell, on July 18th,1901, near Iron Mountain, Wyoming, son of Kels Nickell, sheep rancher, who was Thomas Newton's ("River Tom's") brother. Kels Nickell and River Tom were the sons of John Desha Nickell. River Tom was Oscar Nickell's father, my great great Grandfather. The shooting of Willie Nickell made history, including the movie, *Tom Horn.*

Tom Horn was executed the day before his 43rd birthday by hanging in Cheyenne, Wyoming.

WR Nickell, my uncle, was, in fact, able to attend River Tom's funeral, his great grandfather, in 1944. More of this amazing bloodline information will be revealed as my story continues throughout the series of books to follow.

Thomas Newton "River Tom" Nickell.

Born January 18th, 1853, in Matthew, Morgan County, Kentucky

Death March 29th, 1944, Florress, Morgan County, Kentucky

The complete story about Tom Horn & Willie Nickell can be found on the Podcast,

'Legends of the Old West Podcast,' Tom Horn Ep 6-The Murder of Willie Nickell.

Mother had 8 siblings - 5 brothers and 3 sisters – with her being the youngest of the girls. All her siblings have passed away, leaving her as the only survivor at 88 years of age. Now, suffering from advanced Dementia and Alzheimer's, unable to walk due to a fall at my sister's home in 2023, her condition is a tragic reminder of the family's struggles. There is more to this part of life, as you will come to discover.

When I say there is more to that, believe me!!

Mom grew up under a very heavy-handed father, my Paw Paw, who made all the kids work from dawn to dusk on the farm. Farming, in those days, was grueling, with a few mechanical machines to help ease the burden.

The Original Nickell Home. Alonzo & Dora Adams Nickell.

Attending school was a privilege if your chores were complete. Mother had an 8th-grade education, but in her later years went on to get her GED and manicuring license. Life as they knew it was brutal; most of his children either joined the military or married young to leave their homes on the farm.

Her mother, Maw Maw, was a saintly figure whose strength remains inexplicable to this day. She attributed her resilience to her faith, always saying it came *"through the Lord."* Maw Maw raised eight children; even though Paw Paw was there, his parenting did not take effect until he returned home in the evenings, at times **whispering** to his child of choice, *"Go to the willow tree and pick a branch for your whipping."*

When Paw Paw was not toiling away on the farm, he was lost in the depths of his drinking. His return home was marked by chaos and pain; he would stagger in, fueled by liquor, and unleash his rage on Maw Maw or the children. The once-warm family home turned into a place of uncertainty and dread whenever he was around and had been drinking, in the early years.

My one Uncle, they called him *Little Oscar*, passed at the age of 10 at home due to stomach cancer. Mom was deeply attached to him and always cared for him with all her heart. His passing left her devastated as you can imagine, the entire family shattered. Medical treatments back in the day were rare.

After *Little Oscar's* death, Mother left home at 14 and headed for Des Moines, Iowa, where her mother's sister, *Aunt Maude*, lived with her husband and children.

Soon after, Mom began working in a small cafe where she met her husband, *James D,* the owner. They fell in love, and the story took a cinematic turn, the screen fading to black as in the movies, but the reality was far from a fairy tale. Did I mention the part that Mom was just 15 at the time of her marriage, and J.D. was 42!!! I know, right?!? JD was a mover and a shaker, what we now would call a player, eventually settling in Missouri to go on and have a productive farming life in his later years.

When *Max*, my half-brother (who has always felt like a full sibling to me), in later years, asked his father why in the world he would marry his mother at such a young age…

J.D. responded with, *"Son, you don't know the truth. She lied about her age - she said she was 19."* Surprising twist, isn't it? Nevertheless, *J.D.* always remarked that our mother was the most beautiful young woman he had ever laid eyes on. Her beautiful chestnut-shaded hair framed big hazel eyes, and her skin color was as soft and fair as a dove's.

J.D. reminisced, **whispering**, *"And boy, was she nothing less than a spitfire kinda gal!!"* Seems they both were smitten for varied reasons.

J.D. was always dressed to the hilt, with wingtip shoes, a fedora hat, and a stylish car - the real cat's meow. Max came in October 1953, when mom was just 16, living on Maple Street in Des Moines, Iowa. She had sworn never to be mistreated again, escaping what she described as living with her father. The divorce was finalized on Max's 1st birthday, October 1954.

This was the beginning **whispers** of our dysfunctional Family story – or perhaps just the continuation of generations of chaos?

Did you know we all have old spirits/souls? Our ancestral traumas are handed down through our parents' FAWN (you morph yourself into a situation, survival mode), their parent's FAWN, and so on.

FAWN

One of four trauma states. It is one of the four common reactions to stress danger, alongside Fight, Flight, and Freeze. The FAWN response refers to a person's attendance to try to appease or please others in order to avoid conflict, feel safe, or reduce a perceived threat. It often develops as a coping mechanism in individuals who have experienced prolonged trauma or abuse, particularly in relationships where they feel powerless.

When someone is in a "FAWN" state, they might prioritize others' needs over their own to avoid potential harm or rejection. They will suppress their own feelings or desires to keep peace. They become highly attuned to others' emotions and behaviors in an effort to prevent conflict. They struggle with setting boundaries and may have difficulty saying "NO."

The response is rooted in survival, especially in environments where confrontation could lead to more danger or harm. Overtime, it can become a deeply ingrained behavior, often leading to challenges in maintaining healthy relationships or self-care boundaries.

The cycle of dysfunctionality is bred into us until someone breaks it. If you have heard of *Somatic Breath Work*, you will understand.

The Soma+IQ™ Method

This trademark method of somatic breathwork reconnects the power of our mind back to the innate wisdom of the body, offering an experimental and transformational approach to growth and healing. Rooted in neuroscience, their approach uses somatic-based breathwork, bodywork, and coaching techniques to safely identify and address undigested emotions and physical tension laying dominant in the body. By developing somatic sensing skills, individuals move toward clarity and authentic alignment.

www.somaticbreathwork.com

Mom, ever the gypsy she came to be, decided to take Max to Ft Wayne, Indiana. Her brother *BJ* and his wife lived there, as did my *Aunt Mae*, who seemed to be the most stable of all the siblings at that time. I will never forget my *Aunt Mae*, mother's oldest sibling. She was identical to Maw Maw; she carried unconditional love for her family, her family's family, and even her neighbor's family.

Always a revolving door. Her hands were soft and tender, having a constant presence in the kitchen cooking up meals for her five children, all of whom remained in Ft Wayne except for one, 60 years later.

In my early years, the reunions we had in Ft Wayne were unforgettable. Her home was filled with cousins, aunts, and uncles, neighbors, with plenty to drink and eat…then the *"Ho Down"* would start. Music and singing like never before. At times, I could have sworn this was Opry Land.!!

We were blessed to have a few more of these reunions before her passing in the 90's.

Max recalls a time when Mom disappeared for what seemed to be an entire school year. Come to find out, a whole new timeline came into place for her. She had left for Toledo, where my *Aunt Maddie* was living with her only child, Cousin *D.J. Mom* was nearly 19 years of age and moved in with Aunt Maddie and took a job at the *Tomboy Diner* down the street.

Not too far down the street also was the *Paramount Bar* on Summit St. AHHHH… *The Paramount Bar!!!* This was where my parents first laid eyes on each other. You see, back in the day, there was truly little I.D. checking, especially if you were literally a beautiful, well-trimmed, spicy young lady.

Mom & Dad in the Late 1950's.

The owner, who happened to become my uncle (Ummo *Charlie*), introduced them. My father was there just visiting from Gary, Indiana, but no one could have predicted the whirlwind that would unfold over the next 25 years not even I could make this up!

So many Tragic Whipers.

Mom made her way to Gary, Indiana; once she realized *Al Salman* was the man for her, *Max* stayed with *Uncle BJ in Ft Wayne*, a mere 2.5-hour drive. Mom got a job in the Lounge as a barmaid, and my father was part owner. They married on April 12, 1959. No one recalls the name of that bar.

I remember Mom telling me that after the wedding, they had cornbread, pinto beans, and green onions for dinner, sitting on the floor of their tiny apartment above the bar. Like many others, they were poor but so deeply in love.

Picture *Lucille Ball* and *Desi Arnaz*: Mom with now her fiery red hair, and my father, tall, dark, handsome, and accented. Trouble soon began when they both started getting attention while working at the bar. They were an incredibly attractive couple, quick-witted and charming.

When Mom found out she was pregnant, they decided it was time to move out from above the bar as some type of normality needed to happen. They moved to a two-bedroom over a garage apartment, where Max soon came to live with them after. *Ursula,* my only full-blooded sibling, came along in January of 1960.

Max became everything, leading from babysitter, mother, father, to housekeeper and all in between due to my parents working all the time, being it was at "the bar," many nights they returned home with slurry speeches and mismatched footing, continuously arguing. How could they not be? They both worked in a bar and were still living right down the street.

Ursula 5, Max 11 & ME 3.

Life was continuously filled with brutal fights between our parents. This led to so many trips to our Maw Maw's & Paw Paw's. Waiting for Mom's **whisper**, *"get packed, we are leaving!"* That was Mom's safe haven; her mother kept her safe. Parents are supposed to keep you safe, protected, and feel loved at any given time, right? I believe both parents forgot that as time went on.

As I understand it, my father would always come to collect us and take us back home. Love found its way back, but it did not last long. The time had come for a decision: divorce or try to salvage the marriage by moving to *Toledo, Ohio,* where both parents had relatives, mostly cousins, a term used quite loosely in the Arab world, especially for my father. But mom had her middle sister there - *Aunt Maddie*. Now, this woman was the Shiznik (a term I use for the best of the best, bad-ass crazy, or anything extraordinary that needed describing in between). Oh, how I loved her; she was spicier than even her baby sister!!!

Once settled, my parents wasted no time in buying a business…ha! Another bar! Is anyone catching a common denominator here? This bar was *"The Paramount Bar."* My father bought out his brother-in-law, Ummo Charlie, who was ready to return to Palestine.

Then, the move came to a real house/home. The small white two-bedroom house at 160 Spencer Street became my birthplace on September 26, 1961, at 4:55 a.m. in *Mercy Hospital, Toledo, Ohio.*

Though I have no memories of that home, it still stands. I visited my birth home with my cousin DJ not long ago, still no memories other than mother telling me in later years she was extremely unhappy there. DJ, like us, endured life's wild ride and still grapples with his own struggles, he enlisted in the Marines at just 18 and served in the Vietnam War. Though he survived, now in his 70s, one can not help but wonder—did he truly? Agent Orange has cast a long shadow over more than half of his life. Thank you for your service, cousin!!!

Chaos continued; an example would be Aunt Maddie's husband and DJ just a mere child, with this man not being DJ's father. I will not give any recognition to this person as he rots in jail; I would say he is dead by now. He decapitated a woman, then continued to dismember her – 30 minutes after my Aunt Maddie managed to escape from him. Looking back and hearing the full story, I now realize that her escape was nothing short of a Godwink!

Godwink: An event seemingly coincidental but coming from divine origin

~ Squire D. Rushnell ~

Life went on with both parents working at the bar while Max took care of us girls. Yet, the arguments lingered in the air, making it thick and suffocating. Another opportunity knocked on their doors, a new move to 587 South St. I was only 3, again the younger years of this home I have little recollection, other than what family members have told me. I did return to that home in my 20's for a brief period of time. More on that as we continue on.

It has been said that a child's first memory will dictate to them throughout their lives.

~ Herman Ebbinghaus ~

My first memory was while we still lived in Toledo Ohio. It was a very dark, chilly, rainy night. I remember a two-story red brick building where my mother rushed my sister and me up the stairs to her friend's house, *Windy*. We all were petrified; I will never forget the look on her face when we all started hearing my father yelling from outside, *"Rhoda, come down here and bring the girls. I am going to kill you if you don't come down here right now."*

There was a lot of yelling going on continuously with my mother not muttering a word, not wanting my father to know we were there. Windy scurried us down the backfire staircase and ***whispered*** to us to *"stay under the stairs and up against the wall."*

With my mother's arms around each of us, we crouched down with our heads down, trying not to get more wet than we already were. My father was still yelling upstairs, Windy finally telling him we were not there.

"Go away, you are waking my children," Windy had twin girls, *Rita & Rhoda.* She threatened to call the police. Upon hearing that, he left, only to go home and set my mother's clothes on fire.

As young children, we may not always remember specifically the entire event, but we do remember emotions and images and are often reminded of situations that caused us to be traumatized and lead to being alcoholics, drug addicts, or any other mental illness that attacks our well-being. This, unfortunately, was the beginning of my traumatized life.

At just three years old, I went through something that deeply affected me and shaped my early years in ways I could not fully grasp at the time.

I have pictures of us when we lived on South Street. At times, I am sure we were happy; I remember an Easter Sunday there because we got new dresses and shoes, I have seen pictures of Max, Ursula, DJ, and myself taken there...but no memories. I believe I have to this day I have blocked several of these memories out, to protect my mental state. Did I know or hear of God yet? Not really.

Eventually, time ran out for us in Toledo, Ohio. After a break-in at *The Paramount Bar,* my father told police who he thought it was. At that point, my parents faced another choice: try to salvage their marriage or part ways. **Trauma 1 age 3**

Chapter Two

FAMILY MOVE TO YOUNGSTOWN, OHIO

———⦿———

Still in love, truly, madly, and deeply, I say that with all definitions in mind and noting that Toledo was a top spot for mobsters from all nationalities as well. Then came the robbery of *The Paramount Bar*!

Given my father's minimal years in the States at this time, personally, I believe a decision had to be made and get closer to his people. Either *Cleveland* or *Youngstown, Ohio.* With everything they could pack into and on top of the car, and us three kids inside, they set off heading south.

When they reached a fork in the road, they faced a crucial decision: should they turn right toward *Cleveland, Ohio,* or left toward *Youngstown, Ohio?* And then left it was. I do not remember Mother having any family there that I recall or remember visiting that did not have a couple-hour drive. However, you can bet my father had *"cousins."* Max told me we had a grocery store called the *Golden*

Gate. I have no recollection of that. What I do remember is the grocery store called the *U-Save Market*, and us living at *The Kennedy Park Apartments.*

Although it was not the worst neighborhood, it certainly left much to be desired. I remember fun play times, Max being utterly mean to Ursula and me, always scaring us, or the worst was him sitting on top of us, tickling us so intensely that we often ended up wetting our pants from laughter and fear. He would always want us to say, Uncle!! How could we? We couldn't breathe from laughing and crying so hard. Yeah, Max was no saint back in the day, but it was always sad when he would go to see his father, JD, for the summer; Ursula and I lost without him and usually ended up on the farm.

The first summer in Youngstown, our Maw Maw came to care for us. Leaving the farm and my Paw Paw to fend for himself was hard for her; even with all the children gone, she always took care of Paw Paw. After that first summer, we would go to the farm so Maw Maw could care for Paw Paw, as well as us kids.

During the school year, we would be picked up and go straight to the store, where mom would stick us behind the meat counter that had a huge glass case in front of us; this would potentially keep us safe from all the rift rafts that shopped there.

Before long, *'The Hub Club'* neighborhood tavern, a mere block away, came to be the *"spot."* It was there that my mother taught me to dance on top of the bar and sing *'Cotton Fields,'* and of course, I would earn a bit of spare change from the customers. Ursula stayed mostly with my father at the store. How great was that at only five years old!!

Years later, in my 50's, I asked my mother why she had encouraged me to dance in the bar and sing 'Cotton Fields,'? she flatly called me a liar. However, as I began to describe the dimly lit interior of The Hub Club—the dusty old jukebox in the corner, the worn wooden bar with its cracked leather stools, and the faded neon sign above the door—her eyes widened in disbelief.

The air grew thick with tension, and she nearly fell over from the shock. After a moment of pulling herself together, she looked at me with a mixture of confusion and denial and said,

"I have no idea why you would make this up.!"

As most of us with a traumatic upbringing, we do not want to admit to the crazy things we did, let alone subject our children to them. Even though I have asked several times, Mother never has come clean on this particular event.

Seemed as though life was fairly good for the most during those years. My father would come home after 14/16-hour days working in his store, sometimes his feet literally bleeding. Ursula, myself, and even Max, at times, had to get the tub of soapy hot water and have my father soak his feet while we washed them and then used a menthol cream to rub them out.

At times, my father would about come flying out of that recliner yelling, *"Inna Onna Abouch Aboutizic* (very ugly Arabic swear words), *what's the matter with you? Stop hurting me."*

I was definitely afraid of just his voice, let alone trying to go in for another round. I was then gentle; however, I was giggling inside. I was able to get even for us having to wash his feet every single night. Ha!

A definite trait all my kids learned oh too well as they grew up. Now I understand how those foot rubs were so particularly important. They literally gave us relief from the pain of being on our feet every day with no choice but to rise again the next day to face hard labor once again. My father was absolutely the best provider a family could ever ask for. We had all we needed and definitely all that we wanted. My mother worked like a dog right beside him every day. After having so many lost years and taking time to work through my childhood traumas, I believe whole-heartedly that both parents did the best they could with what and how they were taught and lived in their early years.

The Hub Club continued to play a significant role in our lives as well. To the extent that I was not clear at that tender age, eventually, I was given more truth about the events at the Hub Club; I will be sharing these at a later date in this series of books.

My *Aunt Maddie* & her husband followed us to Youngstown with the understanding my father would put them into their own grocery store. Aunt Maddie worked diligently as always; her husband, well, was just a flat-out user and an evil person to the core. This understanding did not happen as my father, after only a few months, told my aunt and her husband that there was no store for them. Her husband was a lowlife who could not be trusted. Aunt Maddie left him and took herself and her son DJ back to Toledo.

Growing up as a daughter of *Fateeh A. Salman* (referred to as "the godfather, or Big Al") was important back in the day. We always had a few Arabs or a lot of Arabs and their families at our home for dinner. Dinners were always and still are big events in the Arab community. We would have people at the apartment, especially late at night, as all the Arabs had to close their stores up at night. So, it was nothing for people to start arriving at 10/11 pm to break bread.

Discussing overseas connections and their families, there was my father, always ready to strike a deal for anyone with family wanting to come to the United States. He would set them up in some small neighborhood store to start them off. Not sure what his cut was, but you can bet it was not just for a favor. *Fateeh Al Salman* was a business tycoon. One night I will never forget, my brother Max was still with us, and there was a knock at the door.

Mom yelled out, *"Is he alive?"*

Max was to keep an eye on Ursula and me while my mother went to Saint Elizabeth Hospital. My father had been shot with a shotgun in the parking lot of our apartments that night, 25 pieces of buckshot in the right shoulder.

The only way he survived this was as he closed his car door; he saw the reflection of the man holding the shotgun in his back window; he ducked. My aunt Maddie's husband knew that my father always brought the store money back home, usually in a brown paper bag under his coat; you see, my father really was not big on banks quite yet. Seemed this man thought a drive to Youngstown would be prosperous for him.

There were always two stories, one being this attempted murder came from higher up (mobsters) in Toledo due to my father telling the police who robbed him. My father feared no one, ever! The other would-be Maddie's husband, looking for revenge. These two stories could be one and the same. We will never know. The shooter was never captured, and from what I had already shared with you earlier, Aunt Maddie's husband was eventually captured and convicted for the murder and decapitation of a woman in Toledo.

As I understand it, my father crawled, dragging himself on the ground to the first apartment, which was, in fact, Arab but not from our family name. They would not allow my father to come in out of fear; they did call an ambulance. How shameful was that for this Arab man not to help another, especially one of your own kind!!! I am not sure of this, but knowing my father, this man more than likely failed in his business.

Chapter Three

PALESTINE

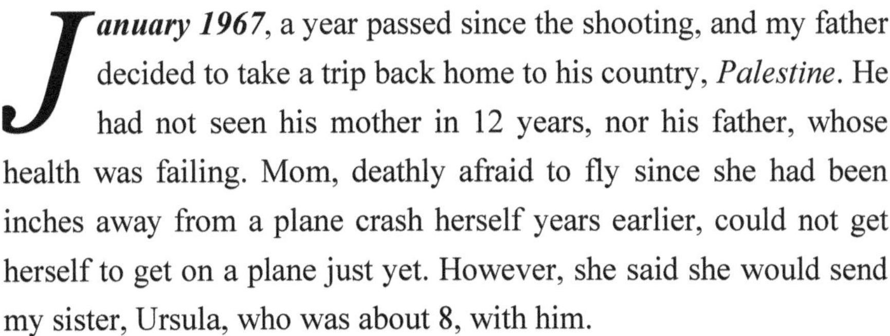

January 1967, a year passed since the shooting, and my father decided to take a trip back home to his country, *Palestine*. He had not seen his mother in 12 years, nor his father, whose health was failing. Mom, deathly afraid to fly since she had been inches away from a plane crash herself years earlier, could not get herself to get on a plane just yet. However, she said she would send my sister, Ursula, who was about 8, with him.

Max was about 14, but he had already decided to stay living with his father in Missouri. I desperately wanted to go; I wanted to be with my father, but I was told I was too young. What? Too young? Ursula and I were only 16 months apart!! This was a three-week trip. They left and returned with no incident…

Other than me having to listen to Ursula getting to ride in a helicopter, and how great everybody was, and getting to meet our grandparents, cousins, and relatives. No doubt Ursula was already a Princess, given she had the beauty of a perfect Arab girl with long, beautiful brunette hair, olive skin, and big brown eyes. Most importantly, she had the name of *"Salman."*

Life continued with what we knew as normal. Parents working, Max gone, mother going into her rages on Ursula and me. I can remember vividly mother going into a rage over one of us girls marking on our bedroom dresser mirror in crayon. I wrote my sister's name, I wanted to get her in trouble...I was so always envious of her even at such an early age, especially with her having to get to a trip with my father overseas. Neither one of us would fess us up to it. Mother went and got a sewing needle and told us to stick our tongues out (like idiots) we complied only to have our tongues pricked with the needle for lying!! Who does this?

Mother finally asked us both where the crayon was that was used on the mirror. I very quickly said *"it is in the top draw."* Mother's wrath was not to be taken lightly, I received one of the worse whippings at the time I thought in my life. I ran outside only to then realize she was right behind me with the belt chasing me. The closer she got the hard the lashing with the belt I felt. A neighbor woman, Ruth, saw this from her window and yelled for me to run to her. I wasted no time in doing that. Mom was not allowed to come in. Eventually, she calmed down, I went home and sent straight to my room...thank God!

It was 1948 when *Israel* with the *United Nations,* approval and authority, declared independence. The government now made a claim for all territory, including *Jerusalem,* previously known as a *Palestinian Territory.*

The opposing countries, such as *Egypt* and *Jordan,* sent in troops, but the Israelis were too powerful. Although the United Nations did try to keep the peace for over two decades, continuous wars broke out over the trade routes, small and large global politics, and then the Israelis went on to claim Jerusalem—events leading up to what eventually was known in the history books as the ***Six-Day War in 1967.***

It was early February 1967 when I heard I was going overseas. I was thrilled! My parents were sending me back home to visit!! How could this be? Was my father showing favor to me? Will I never know?

Eventually, years later, when I asked my mother, *"Why did you send me alone, with one of dad's cousins that I barely knew?"* Her response was the one I will never forget.

She said, *"We wanted one of you girls raised in America and one of you girls raised overseas the Palestinian way."*

Was that supposed to satisfy this life-antagonizing question?

Off I go with *Fiaz,* I would call him Ummo (Uncle) out of respect. It was a long flight, 24 hours door to door. The airplane was like nothing I could have even imagined. It was a 747 Jumbo jet, with a winding staircase taking you to the top floor of the Jet.

I was treated like a princess by the flight attendants and given the full tour, including the cockpit, where the captain gave me a set of flight wings. This was going to be the best trip ever!! Until it was not...

We arrived at Tel Aviv airport. Greeted by Israeli authorities, I was separated from Fiaz. I was taken into a small room. There were no windows to look outside, only the small window in the door, made of steel.

A female Israeli militant came into the room. She was questioning me, asking me my name, my father's name, where I was going, and who I was going to see there. She also wanted to know who the man was with me. Well, clearly, I knew almost all the answers except for Fiaz's last name, nor did I know my grandparent's names other than *Sitee* and *Seedo*. I was detained for what seemed to be hours.

They had me remove my clothes, except for panties and the spaghetti strap undershirts little girls wore back then. With my clothes, they took my shoes and my camera. They then proceeded to pull all the film out of my camera and pull the souls out of my shoes while my other clothes had been taken somewhere else.

Eventually, my clothes were returned with my suitcase, and I was free to go, just like that. I don't even think I knew what was going on; I just knew something was not right. I was afraid, and I knew it had to do something with my father. Later years, I came to find out my father had been quite an influence in the P.L.O *(Palestinian Liberation Organization),* and since I was his daughter, there was no reason for the Israelis not to think I was a carrier for my father in bringing something valuable to the P.L.O.

Back in those days, from reliable resources I was reminded that my father sent suitcases of cash overseas. At times, I do remember seeing these suitcases passed along to a cousin who was leaving for overseas, but not until later years that I realized most of this was to support the P.L.O. As well as hiding cash from the government and my mother.

I now was settled with my Umptie Nejah and her children. My Ummo Charlie had moved back to Palestine after my father had bought him out from the Paramount Bar in Toledo, Ohio. I started attending school there at the *Friends Girls School* in *Ramallah*. There was *The Friends Boys School* as well.

Both schools wore uniforms, had strict rules, and were not allowed to intermingle until the 11th and 12 grades. We walked to school every day. My cousins protected me well and always made sure I was at the gates of school before going to their side of the campus.

Spring of 1967, Egyptian President *Gamal Abdul Nasser* requested the U.N.'s personal removal of Israeli Ships. The president also mobilized troops to the *Sani Peninsula* and blocked Israeli ships, many of which traveled through the *Strait of Iran*. More so to irrupt Israelis' safety and in hopes of eliminating that country and reclaiming their own land.

May 17, 1964: The *Palestinian Liberation Organization (P.L.O)* was founded during a Summit in Cairo, Egypt. Their initial goals were to bring together various Arab groups to create a liberated Palestine in Israel. In time, the P.L.O. took on a larger role, claiming to represent all the Palestinians while running the *Palestinian National*

Authority (P.N.A.). In the beginning, the P.L.O. was initially not known to be violent in the early years, but they were associated with controversial tactics, terrorism, and extremism.

Military leader *Yasser Arafat* led a group known as *Fatah*. The Palestinians lacked formal leadership. Yasser Arafat began to infiltrate the P.N.C., becoming the Chairperson of the now P.L.O. Executive Committee, holding this title until his death in November of 2004.

Hamas was formed in 1987 during the first Palestinian uprising, also known as the *Intifada*. This group was committed to armed resistance against Israel and working towards the creation of an Islamic Palestinian state instead of Israel. Fatah was a descendant of a Palestinian organization, now inactive due to the upcoming events. The *Fatah-Hamas* conflict fought against one another for power, leading to Hamas's takeover of the *Gaza Strip* in 2007.

In April 1967, Syria backed Palestinian guerrillas and began small attacks. These attacks led to a serious battle between Syria and Israel, leaving six Syrian fighter jets destroyed. On May 22, *President Gamal* banned Israeli ships from entering the *Straights of Tiran,* the passage connecting the *Red Sea in the Gulf of Aqaba.*

A week later, his defense was signed with *King Hussein* of Jordan due to false reports of an *Egyptian* victory Mid May, *Egypt*, along with *Syria, Jordan*, and *Iraq*, soon following increased military forces along Israeli shared borders.

American President *Lyndon Baines Johnson (LBJ)* cautioned both sides not to fire the first shot and asked for support in reopening the

Straights of Tiran. Unfortunately, this plan did not materialize. But forced the hand of Israel and simultaneously launched air attacks. The first strike was a success, decimating Egyptian air forces, Jordan then was overmatched.

On June 7, 1967, the United Nations called for a cease-fire. Israel had claimed Old Jerusalem, where most Israelis celebrated by praying at the *Damascus Gate/Western Wall* in Jerusalem. Jordan accepted a cease-fire at once.

The Wailing Wall Damascus Gate, East Jerusalem.

On ***June 8, 1967***, Egypt accepted, on ***June 10, 1967***, Syria accepted, and on ***June 11, 1967,*** the war ended. Hundreds of thousands were captured and put into Israeli concentration camps; over 800 Israeli troops were killed as well. Israel claimed more territory than the already 7200 miles they owned before the war, which was less than 2% of the *Middle East*. Victory for Israel, a young, small nation!!

The Gaza Strip, the Sani Peninsula, The Golden Heights from Syria, and the West Bank from Jordan, including Jerusalem, were all now considered Israeli territory.

By *August of 1967*, wounded by default in the six-day war, Arab leaders met in *Khartoum, Sudan,* signing papers promising *"No Peace, No Recognition and No Negotiations with Israel."* However, in 1982, Israel did return the Sinai Peninsula to Egypt as part of a peace treaty, and then in 2005, they withdrew from the Gaza Strip.

On *November 13, 1974*, at 10:30 am, *Yasser Arafat was recognized by the United Nations as the sole representative of the Palestinian people—the P.L.O.* My father had a long-time family friend, Nasser, orchestrate a bus to go from Youngstown to Washington, DC, to rally for our lost country. The last I remember was seeing the doors close behind my father as Arafat had invited him to join him and his entourage of security.

Arafat began his speech with:

"Today, I have come bearing an olive branch and a freedom fighter's gun. Do not let the olive tree branch fall from my hand; I repeat, do not allow the olive branch to fall from my hand."

Most of the delegates and state representatives who were not familiar with Palestinian culture missed the analogy of the olive branch and freedom fighter's gun as a significant symbol of Palestine.

The olive trees over the years were associated with indigeneity:

A quality of a person's and a group's identity that links them to specific places with knowledge and respect for original ways.

Therefore, *Israel* cut as many trees down as they could and replaced them with pine trees. Before the founding of Israel, *The Jewish National Fund (J.N.F.)* planted *Aleppo Pines* to claim land for the Jewish state. If it were not developed within ten years, it would be returned to its earlier owners. Therefore, trees were used as a stand-in when settlers were not available.

Over the years, due to the success of negotiations, in 1994, *Yasser Arafat,* along with *Prime Ministers Rabin and Peres*, received the *Nobel Peace Prize.*

Now, back to 1967, when I experienced the *historical* **Six-Day War**. I was already begging to go home. With shivers down my spine, I was so afraid. Daily, we would hear and feel the aftermath of bombs exploding while being intimidated by Israeli soldiers who stood on top of buildings with their machine guns.

The Israelis had a concentration camp right across from my Umptie Nejeh's home. Our city was now considered the first city in the *West Bank* to be occupied territory - *El-Bireh, Ramallah.*

Our Family home, El-Bireh Ramallah. First Occupied City in the West Bank.

31

The most terrifying traumatic memory was being in class, and all of a sudden, we heard machine guns go off, and Israeli soldiers were penetrating the schools, telling everyone to get out.

The soldiers had no mercy, even on us as young children. If it had not been for Dania, a friend of one of my cousins who knew who I was, I would have been dead. She saw a soldier coming towards me; I was frozen in my spot. Dania bravely covered me with her body, leaving her backside open for what was to come next. The butt of the gun thrusting into her back, no doubt broken; I remember her **whispering** to me, *"Run Deana, go hide habibti." (Habibti; Term of Endearment)*

I did do just that, crouched down in another building, crying, petrified. Then, hearing my cousin calling my name (Nejeh's youngest daughter), found me, and we scurried home. We lived about a 30-minute walk from our school in *Ramallah* to our town, *El-Bireh*. We ran all the way. It seemed like hours that it took us to get home that day.

The city was amuck. Such confusion and talk about what has happened. I just wanted to go home to America. I can remember begging my parents to bring me home, writing letters asking mom to send our dog, Ben, over so I could ride on his back home. I used to always ride on his back. He was so big.

I, at six years of age, had no idea the geographics of my location. You see, Ben was our German Shepard, titled *"Sir Ben Salman of Jordan."* The cousins always comment how they would love to be Fateeh's dog. *'He eats a steak every night!'* Oh, how we loved that dog for many years until finally, he crossed over the rainbow in the early 70's.

I was beaten by my Ummo Mofeed on several occasions. Both bio-aunties tried to block him whenever they could; even his wife would come to protect me from his wrath. He had found one of the letters I wrote home, begging to come home. Ummo took this as an insult, needless to say, and an embarrassment to *Salman*, a good name, his name in particular.

In **March 1968**, I was admitted back into the United States of America upon the United Nations requesting all American citizens to return home.

The war at this time was ongoing—surprise attacks/ demonstrations from both sides at any given moment.

Not to mention, my mother's side of the family was beginning to grow upset with her for not bringing her baby home. What was she thinking?

Did she not want me? She did not! Eventually, confessing to me.

Trauma 3 age 7.

On the positive side, my mother told me that they could not bring me home sooner because they had such a major surprise and wanted it to be perfect when I returned. We now owned our own home on Coitsville Hubbard Rd, *Coitsville, Ohio*.

Normality was on the rise; I just knew it!

Chapter Four

ANNIE COMES TO OHIO

—⚬⦿⚬—

Now life was going to be normal!! One of the most incorrect statements I have ever made!!!!

Not long after moving to our new home, I was sent two doors down to get a pack of smokes for Mom, Virginia Slims, to be exact. Back then, you did not need an ID, especially when this was a... wait, what? An Arab cousin's corner grocery store!! Shocking, right?

This one particular day like any other, I went to fetch her smokes. - I was always there for something: smokes, milk, bread. You know, the simple things. However, on this day, I noticed one of the brothers, *Amjed*, was not in sight. I asked about him, and his brother *Khalad* said that he was probably in the walk-in cooler.

Next thing I know, we both hear a pop, with a black young man having his hand around my cousin's throat, gun to head, blood everywhere, with another black young man holding a gun and also keeping a lookout in order to rob the store.

My cousin Khalad yelled for me to run! I knew where the back door was, so I bolted toward it, hearing footsteps close behind. With no time to think, I slipped into the cooler and waited - what felt like forever, **whispering** to myself, *"God please save me"!* I did know how NOT to lock myself in, probably from doing just that so many times in past stores. I carefully pushed the big steel door open, looked cautiously, and when I didn't see anyone again, I bolted. I had to cross the back of the store to the other side to get to the back door. Suddenly, I heard my cousin yelling, *"Call the police, ya Deana, call the police."* I couldn't help but find myself being angry and even more scared that my cousin was reminding the robbers I was still there, and they now knew my name! Hoping no one was chasing me, I sprinted to the first house between the store and mine. I threw myself into the ditch, waiting for a sign it was safe to move again.

Then I heard it—the car screeched away. I took off, barely able to breathe, but I had to get home and tell my mother what had happened.

I finally was able to mutter, *"Amjed was just shot."* Two black guys came in and grabbed Amjed by the neck from behind, and then they shot him while bringing him to the front of the store where Khalad was.

When we saw police arriving, lots of them, mom took me back over to the store. Blood everywhere…a memory still embedded in my head to this day. I was interviewed, they tell me, although I have no memory of this. I remember everything up to telling my mother what had happened and then going back to the store, blood everywhere!!!

After that, it was completely blank, like a clean slate, without a speck of ink. I do not remember any of the criminal questioning or investigation. What I find tremendously insane now is that I was literally begging my parents to send me back home to Palestine after I was told I was going to have to testify. TESTIFY!!!

Being very relieved that Amjed survived—thank you, *Lord*! —and Khalad's testimony, the robbers took a plea deal at the 11th hour as I sat outside of the courtroom, hoping no one related to the criminals recognized me or tried to remember my face.

Time passed; I was safe. **Trauma 4 age 8**

Honestly, could life please be a bit less cruel? I was only eight years old and faced the fourth trauma of my life!! Had I even thought much about God? Talking to HIM? Only when I was in trouble, like most warm or non-believers. Also, I knew of the Islamic religion practiced by my father's family on a regular basis; My father did not.

As of then, the only religion I could remember was my Maw Maw reading her bible daily and going to revivals regularly. It has been told that even when my Paw Paw was a drinker, he would put Maw Maw on the back of his horse and take her up to the church house. Revivals could go on for days. It was the craziest thing as a child I ever saw; let's go with Pentecostal, talking in tongues, dancing in the spirit, you name it.

Time passed, and life resumed to normal – the constant arguing between my parents, our frequent escapes to the farm, and always returning home. For a brief while, a blissful peace hovered over our home, waiting to slip away.

Then, one day, coming home from school to Ursula's and to my surprise, a blue convertible with a white top was in our back drive.

You see, with this house in Coitsville, you didn't just pull in; you had to drive up a very long drive with aged, enormous evergreen trees on both sides, with a metal fence gate opening to a huge 4 square parking lot, closing the gate at night was always one of our chores after my father was home, if we were still awake, or he would close it. We reopened in the mornings when we left for school.

Two gals were in the house with both my parents there. These gals were straight out of the 60's - black eyeliner, bleached blonde hair, smokers, and mouths like sailors. One of these girls was my half-sister. Yes, my sister! *Annie* (Fatimeh) was here in Ohio.

My sister and I shared several events in common. We shared the same birthdays, September 26, 1951, and mine in 1961. Annie was my father's first bio child, a girl, and I was his last bio child, a girl, separate mothers, ten years to the day apart. I do not even remember hearing about her at all until that day.

Turns out, I have a half-brother too—Freddy, or *Fuad* in Palestinian. He was younger than Annie. She was 18, and he was 16, still in school. You see, Freddy fell behind after a horrible accident at the age of only five years old. He and his cousin were playing with a bow and arrows. Apparently, one of the tips came off the arrow.

His cousin shot an arrow, and without knowing the arrow tip had fallen off, Freddy walked right into the line of fire with the arrow landing straight into his left eye. This left him blind in that eye, creating brain damage that caused him to stutter and mentally not completely able to comprehend. Moving forward, Annie always stayed close to him and protected him, including beating the snot out of several bullies at their school whenever necessary.

In 1949, my father landed in Gary, Indiana, after being released from *Ellis Island*. He had cousins there; you always go to cousins when you hit the United States. A mutual friend soon introduced him to a woman named *Lib*. Lebanese as could be, to include all the greed and hatefulness some of these women would carry through life with them.

Arrangements were made for my father to marry her oldest daughter, *Judith*. She was so young and innocent at the tender age of 16 that she was made to quit school in the 9th grade and marry my father for the enormous amount of ONLY $500—another mother who allowed her child to be sold off for the love of money.

They had two children together, *Annie* and *Freddy*, but soon after the green card came, the card of cards…which meant you were legal to stay in the United States, my father left Judy. By this time, my father had met my mother in Toledo and fell in love for the first time at the early age of 29; my mother, being a young, spicy, flirtatious redhead, moved to Gary, Indiana, and they married there. *Ursula* came along in January of 1960.

Annie & Max eventually came to live them them as well. Freddy never did bond with my father, but as I understand from Max & Cousin DJ, Freddy always visited. So naturally, all they ever heard from Judy was how my father left them to fend for themselves. In later years, I did have confirmation that my father sent child support every single month; in fact, for the remaining balance of Freddy's 17th year, my parents took a note out at the bank to pay it in one lump sum just to rid themselves of Judith's wrath.

After Annie graduated from high school and was now over 18, she wanted to see her father and seek out some truths. She already despised her mother at the time; she was a very hateful woman in nature, as I was told, who lived on the memory of my father being a mean and cruel man and leaving them!! I often wondered, truly, my children's take on my divorces from their fathers.

I can humbly say I believe my children when they say, *"Mom, we love you and honor all you did for us. You did what you could with what you had."* Whewww, this is a song to a divorcee's ears, especially when you read about what comes to pass in forward years.

Annie told us that her mother brainwashed both her and her brother against my father, and definitely about my mother, stealing her husband and then leaving both kids behind. Annie stayed behind, as she could not leave her brother, Freddy.

The girls stayed for about a week, going out partying every night, which made my father especially crazy. So, he and my mother came up with the idea (not sure how much mother had to do with it, what *Fateeh* says goes in our home for the most) that Annie come live with us. Knowing my father, he made it sound like a dream come true, especially if you are promised your own convertible Mustang and freedom from a mean mother. I get it!

The girls left back to *Valparaiso, Indiana,* where Annie's mother had moved to after she remarried and lived there for years, up until she died in 2017. It was not long before Annie returned by bus with all her belongings, which mainly consisted of makeup and some too-tight seductive clothes.

The shopping sprees began, and the makeup calmed down a bit, but she never went anywhere without her eyes on—her trademark till death. Eventually, she got the car promised to her, a convertible Mustang. Yellow with black trim, she was a real beauty and attention grabber.

Along with the car came the understanding that she would go to meat-cutting school and learn the trade of becoming a butcher. My father was no dummy; he always said, *"Do not start something that you do not know how it's going to end."* He was setting himself up, as well as his store, for success with his own blood in-house butcher, and Annie was the perfect fit with her being a strong, hefty young woman.

Time passed, and her school was completed. She started working in the store, the U Save market. She also became my mother's personal maid. Seems the more time Annie lived with us, the more chores my mother had for her after work. Was my mother jealous? There was something there, not sure why, other than my mother could definitely be the most unloving person at times. It literally was like living with *Dr. Jekyll and Mr. Hyde*.

Eventually, in November of 1970, Annie being just 19, my father announced he wanted to take Annie overseas and introduce her to the *family* and discussed the possibility of marriage. Now remember, because of her mother's bloodline, she was more Arab than Ursula and I. Off they went, with suitcases of cash, dad on a mission. Annie, being my father's daughter, looked for the approval and love of our father and yet still the profit in all this. Definitely first blood!

Mahmoony (Mike) was his name. I never could understand why she would do this. I get it if you are already living overseas, but she went to marry willingly… kinda. From the picture it is clear she was not genuinely happy.

ANNIE's Marriage Walk through the streets of El-Bireh with my father on the left and his brother Ummo Mofeed 1970.

Before Annie left, she confided in my mother about her virginity status. She did not know what to do. After all these years, at 63, I recently discovered who was behind saving Annie from a horrific beating or killed when her non-pureness was confirmed - my mother, of all people! I had always believed that Annie came up with it on her own.

A long-time friend of the family, *Lyn*, In Toledo, whom I recently interviewed, said my mother told her about this situation, and she told

Annie what to do. Okay, I am not going to go into 100 more pages of WOW!!! On the night of consummation, the Arab women would stand outside of the *gorfanoom* (Bedroom); *they would wait silently until the bride brought them her sheets, confirming virginity.*

Annie was instructed to slit her upper thigh with a razor, bleed on sheets, let her husband see, and then take the sheets to the women for celebration - a tradition that carries on till this day.

"Wow, mom, really? You do have compassion!!! They all returned to America. Mike & Annie had a house just a block away from the U Save Market. Mike was to take over the store, Annie was naturally the butcher, and all was working out, until it did not.

Annie was just five months pregnant when my father granted them a divorce. Mike was an absolute piece of work! He would beat Annie even while pregnant and still working. Mike rarely worked the store; he was a womanizer and loved to gamble, he wanted to be my father!! How delusional is that? NO ONE COULD BE THAT MAN—so many layers to Fateeh. My father had moved on to a bigger store, so he really had no idea of all that was going on.

Finally, Annie confided in him. He granted a divorce at once. She moved in with us, continuing to work; Mike, now out of the picture entirely with a ruined name, moved to Chicago. It was decided to have the baby adopted out.

Annie surely did not and was not ready to be a mother. Eventually, my father came to accept the offer from his attorney that he and his wife would adopt the baby gladly. A Jewish couple…go figure!

All was set! Annie and I shared my 10th and her 20th birthday together that year. She used to, and still did to the day of her passing, say laughingly, *"I can't even have my own damned birthday."*

I loved her so much, especially through my years to come with serious addiction, with no judgment from her. I could call her at any time, and she would talk me down. Annie was two weeks overdue; this particular night, my mother made an announcement.

"We are not adopting this child out; we are keeping her!!"

That evening, Labor began, and *Dana* was born. *Godwink*! Oh, how my mother and father loved her. I, on the other hand, lost my place in the family legacy. I was no longer the baby of our family. It was all about *Dana*! I can still remember to this day when Dana was brought home. Clearly, Mom had given this prior thought, and I was given a *Miss Beasley* doll. Do you remember her? You could pull her string, and she would talk like a child, asking to be fed and diapered as well. She had one of those bottles that you could insert through a small hole in her mouth and feed her—then burb and diaper.

Mom said to me, *"This is your baby now to take care of, and Dana is ours to take care of."*

What? Seriously? Had I just been replaced by a 12-inch cloth doll? I most certainly was.!! **Trauma 5 age 10**

We even ended up giving away our family dog of years, a French poodle named *FiFi*, as she became a recluse, she would hide under the bed, and she started snapping at people. This was so out of character for her. So, as my mother seemed to be able to do easily…she gave her away. This broke my heart - FiFi & I was disposable.

Three years or so went by, tensions grew between my mother and Annie; while my father had a live toy, *Dana*, that he would always love on, play with, and give much attention to. My brother Max did tell me while interviewing him about my childhood, that he could remember my father doing the same with me, that I was his pride and joy.

Personally, I think my father was just that way with young children. They love unconditionally and rarely rebel, which made it easy for my father. Eventually, my parents adopted *Dana* when she was around three years old.

You can bet that Annie was thrilled to have that "*motherhood*" pressure off. However, Mahmoody's name was muddled big time since he had to sign off as well. There is absolutely no doubt that he was given a very handsome amount of cash along with his signature to walk away, and also, there is this: *you get to live!!*

As a couple of years rolled on, Mahmoody started contacting my father, talking about putting a better life together for him and Annie and asked about Dana joining the family again as well. That was a flat-out NO WAY. Moving forward, Annie agreed to see Mahmoody again, only due to her exhausting life in our home. He came to Youngstown from Chicago, where he now lived and owned a grocery store with his brother. Annie weighed her choices, and she chose Mahmoody. He and Annie re-married right there in our living room in Coitsville, and off they went.

She could now escape the wrath of my mother and having to be the Nanny for *Dana* still. Mom seemed to go through a depression spell and stayed in bed for what seemed like weeks. My sister and I cared for Dana as we could.

Annie said to me later in life, *"It was a very easy decision to leave our father's house and go to Chicago with Mike; I learned to fight back,"* she then **whispered**.

Ursula and I would miss her and the fun times we had.

With that being said, I must tell one last story about Annie and us girls and the crazy that Annie always created. This particular Saturday, Mom and Dad were off to an afternoon event at the country club. Mother always got her hair done the day before the event, and she always had her perfume *Occur by Avon* on to enter the room before her. Indeed, that was Rhoda's signature for years. Have you ever been able to déjà vu with a certain aroma? Is the aroma of your grandmother's apple pie or cornbread cooling down? She eventually moved on to high-end department store options. To this day, whenever Avon has Occur in stock, I make sure to keep a bottle tucked away.

There were carpet remnants all over. Mom had a new carpet put in throughout the house. Conveniently, they would be out for the day, and *"This mess had better be cleaned up by the time we get home."* Mother barked!!!

With her, ordereds were always to do something. Seriously, we knew her wrath would be far from pleasant if a task was not completed exactly as instructed by the dictatorship that ruled our home; it just depended on which dictator was barking the orders at the time. Annie was vacuuming, Ursula picking up remnants, while I crawled on my hands and knees, clearing out the fuzz off the baseboards. I got the crap jobs, Lol.

Ursula would just not let Annie be, and she kept unplugging the vacuum. This was hilarious!! These two always got each other good. Annie reached down and got a carpet remnant strip. She snatched my sister, threw her on the ground, and had that carpet strip around her throat, choking her. After what seemed to be forever, I started yelling at Annie to let her go…SHE IS DEAD!

"You killed her, Annie!!" I am not even exaggerating in this next statement. We both looked square in the eyes, and at the same time, we said, *"What are we going to tell Dad?"*

No thoughts whatsoever crossed our minds to call for help. If any help was needed, it was going to be for Annie & I, actually all Annie. She would have never allowed me even to come close to taking the hit on this.

Ursula started moving around; Annie and I started dancing and crying in relief that we were not going to be killed as well, oh yeah, and that Ursula was alive.

Let us put this in perspective: my only full-blooded sister was either dead or dying, and our most heroic effort was shaking her a few times. No calls for medical help - our biggest worry was,

"What are we going to tell Dad?"

Ursula survived, as well as Annie and me. Ursula used that ace in the hole many times over on Annie, including my boy-crazy sister sneaking boys in the house through the back door and out the front when Annie would call out, *"They are home!!"*

Annie was gone. Life went on. We were moving up in the world. A brick-and-white bi-level house on Willow-Wood Dr was bought in *Liberty*, Ohio, with fancier cars, more Arab *Hafla's* (parties) to attend at the *Nadie* (club), shopping, entertaining home diners, living the good life with consequences. My Uncle CK, a definite OG on the Nickell side would come to the house in the night and leave early mornings. He had already done time for bank robbery, but again on the run from the FBI. On one occasion the FBI coming to our home, surrounding it, then demanding my uncle come out. My father was the only one there as Mom, Ursula and I was already overseas. I loved my uncle CK so very much, he always defended me, and he too held a special place in his heart for me. Later he turned himself in, only to be released early due to health issues, leaving this world, and me way to early.

Ursula and I both had chores naturally, but come on now, we are talking before school, after school, and especially on weekends; we were always at one of my father's stores at any given time, working if there was no school. I remember Ursula and I were always acting out; the trick was not to get caught. On this one day it was my turn to work the store.

I was about 13, and I had taken up smoking, thanks to my mother making me eat cigarettes when I pretended to puff on one as she asked me to get her cigarettes one day. I would hide my cigarettes in the women's bathroom, behind the hot water tank. Safe right? No, not that day.

When I came to work after school, one of the girls that worked for us named, *Esther* told me my father had found my cigarettes. How in the world could he ever have found those cigarettes in the girl's restroom? That would be my biggest question. Esther told me my father had to get to the bathroom, so he went into the women's bathroom and saw that a brick was out of place under the hot water heater. I was so scared I knew I was dead when my father got a hold of me.

Nasser came to the store to visit; he always came when he knew my father was on his way; he cared deeply for my father, not only as an Arab of Palestine but also as a mentor. My father gave him his first chance in America as a store owner. My father, too, cared deeply for Nasser. Nasser, to this day, still fights diligently for *Our Lost People of the Lost Country of Palestine.* I had a slight crush on him, he was very handsome, funny, and always had a genuine heart.

This time, however, I was not interested in trying to flirt with him; I told him my father was going to kill me and that he had found my cigarettes. He said he would talk to him and make it ok. He told me to go to the back, where we kept the produce, and finish my work. I did as he said, with one exception...I laid on the floor like I had fainted.

Waiting for someone to come find me. I am not sure why I did this other than in some crazy way, thinking I would prevent receiving the wrath of my father, even though Nasser was there to soften him up.

One of my coworkers found me. At the exact time, my father had just come into the store, and they ran and got him. He had them call an ambulance. He rode with me to the hospital, and I could remember him **whispering** to me, *"It's okay, yabbah, I know about the cigarettes."*

I did not react, but I heard him say that, and I knew I was no longer in trouble. Whewww, I was safe! Nasser followed behind to confirm I was going to be ok.

But get this, just to show you how unprofessional doctors were back then, this particular Dr. (he has passed since) informed my parents that it was a neurological disorder and that I needed to go into traction. Yes, traction!! There I lay for the next five days with my legs bound with weights on them to help realign my neurological disorder. I was fine with that, off school and work and not in trouble. I was winning in life. That was definitely one of my better pull-offs.

Then came the coupon fraud…not mine, but of the same blood.

My father started his infamous coupon swindle with one of my uncles, Mom's brother, *Frank,* another OG *(Original Gangsta).* This had been going on for some time and now needed more hands to cut coupons. Both Uncle Frank and my father had mostly family members in various cities, and states cutting coupons from newspapers, dampening them, and then tossing them in the dryer to make them look used. They would bundle them up and send them to my father, then in turn he worked them through his grocery stores to be sent to the distribution center in *El-Paso, Texas.* Most family members didn't really get the gist of the scam and thought they were being paid to help support the grocery stores, and the extra income for them was well worth their efforts.

You get reimbursements, one being the cost of coupons discounted to customers, then the small percentage you get as a handler's fee. They had been making bank for years. I am talking millions!!! Great parenting skills, right? Let us teach our kids and relatives how to be part of this enormous federal fraud!! This is how several of the millions my father had sent overseas were acquired, no doubt.

Remember me talking about what my father used to say, *"Don't start something that you can't see to the end?"*

Well, he and my uncle had a silent partner…very silent. His name was never revealed to my knowledge. All he had to do was take the hit when they got busted eventually. They did get noticed and investigated many years later; their scapegoat did his job and served two years with a very handsome income. My father and *Uncle Frank* were untouched. Several more *"transactions"* occurred with my father and the *"Nickell"* brothers over the years to come.

Chapter Five

EL-BIREH RAMALLAH

———————————————⌒◉⌒———————————————

The year was 1974, *El-Bireh Ramallah, Palestine.* I was 13 years of age when I was sent overseas to attend school. It felt like I was always being sent away as if I were being punished for being '*different.*' I was again earlier sent to Palestine at age 11 for a few months, probably for a summer. Not sure why, other than, I was different.

Ursula, Sitee, Dana & Me. El-Bireh Palestine 1974.

You see, I had taken a liking to an Arab gentleman who often visited two doors down. Actually, it was his cousin who lived there, but I would go over all the time to see him. His name was *Munjed*. Since I had a female distant cousin there, it was never questioned why I spent so much time over there.

Munjed would come a couple of times a week and meet me on the back road/alley to pick me up and take me to school as well. Ursula had herself an Arab on the hook as well. He was more of her chauffeur; both men were about 20 years of age.

Munjed's uncle eventually made aware of his feelings for me; Munjed had asked his uncle to approach my family and ask for my hand in marriage. Ugh!!!

But instead of going to my father, his uncle went to my mother. They both decided that this had to end; his nephew was not of the same caliber as our family. His uncle promised to keep it from my father if my mother could put a stop to us seeing each other.

After I was reprimanded, I wrote a letter to Munjed. We always did this; his cousin *Nadia* was our messenger. This event was New Year's Eve. Munjed was at our cousin's house celebrating New Year's Eve. I was waiting for my mother to go to bed so I could get my letter to him; I hid it under my bathroom sink, behind the plumbing. Safe right? Not right! Here comes my mother deciding to clean with her OCD self. Why on New Year's Eve? And why my bathroom?

Once again, I saw my life flash before me. In the letter, I told Munjed of how I had gotten into trouble from his uncle telling on us

- maybe I had talked back - but while my mom was in my bedroom, she grabbed whatever was closest to her (As usual) and started whipping me with it. It was the cord to my hot rollers this time.

When those prongs came tearing into my flesh like a whip, I would just bellow out in agony. Finally, she stopped, and I was to stay in my room to lick my wounds, as she called it. Hence, the letter was written to Munjed.

As mom decided to clean, I was in a panic. Ursula told me to act sick. I was always told to act sick wherever things got out of hand, and this could have been the worst beating yet - especially since I had ratted my mother out to Munjed. So, I followed the plan, and honestly, I could have won an Oscar for my performance since I literally was sick to my stomach knowing what was about to happen and did not have to act much.

The ambulance was called for severe abdominal pain, and Mom and I went to the hospital while Ursula retrieved my letter. Another trump card for her to hold over me, but it was still better than facing the wrath of Rhoda.

Anyhow, here I went again, packing two suitcases, both lined with cash, headed overseas. I had no idea who my escort was this time. But I do know El-Bireh, Ramallah, Palestine, was still considered occupied territory in the West Bank.

Once again, I found myself attending the *Friends Girls School* in *Ramallah*. It was a private school, and overall, it seemed fine. Only the 11th and 12th-grade students were allowed to interact, with girls and boys attending each other's schools—*Friends Boys School*—for the final classes that were not offered at both schools.

Mrs. Tuttle was the school principal, and she was from America - an older woman, soft-spoken, always seemed to care for the best interest of her school. I am not sure what *Mr. Tuttle's* job was, but he always went to the post office, all the girls were excited to see if we received any mail from the states. I remember him getting a real kick out of me singing the song *"Hey Mr. Postman"* every time I saw him coming with the mail.

Of course, I was always known as an *"Amrikie,"* the "American." Even though my father held one of the highest positions with the *Palestinian Liberation Organization* (P.L.O), I had very few friends. Having a father with such influence in the community was not a blessing for sure as a teenager.

Most gals were standoffish. I had one or two friends who, at that time, I thought were friends, but as my story continues, you will see they were not much of a friend. These girls were half-American as well but had lived overseas for several years at this point with both parents; mothers converted to Islam... My friend *Dora* & her sister *Fatima'* lived with family relatives and had been there for some time.

Their father was Palestinian, my father's 2nd cousin and their mother had passed a while back, who was Brazilian. As usual, an Arab man wastes no time collecting another bride, younger and still of childbearing age. Dora & Fatima were left overseas as their father went back to the States (*Oakland, California*) with his new bride and baby on the way. I had become such good friends with Dora and her sister.

Dora and I were inseparable. Eventually when my mother and Ursula came, they lasted a whole five months; however, Mom met Dora and Fatima, and everyone got along so well.

My mother really liked these girls. Dora and I bonded for over a year before they went back home to America; we always made a promise that we would stay in touch; after all, her father was my father's second cousin.

The time came for Dora and Fatima to return to California. Fatima was married while she was still there in Palestine. I cannot recall 100%, but I believe that is why the girls got to go home, and Dora went to live with Fatima and her husband. They both told me many stories about their brother *Miscal*; it became a big ongoing joke that when we all got back to America, they were going to *"fix me up"* with him.

I had seen pictures of him, and he was a nice-looking young man. He was about four years older than me at that time, so he would have been about 18 or 19. He stayed behind and did not come overseas; he was running the family grocery store, as most Arabs had a family grocery store.

Soon after they left, trouble kept finding me, and once again, I was abandoned.

I hated it there—still not accepted as *Fateeh's* daughter—and my rebellion only grew. That is when I began really acting out. I could care less what people thought of me…or did I only want my father's attention?

But always be careful what you wish for, my friends!!! I met a guy named *Amin*; everyone called him *Ace*. He was Arab/British and attended the *Friends Boys School* as a senior.

Eventually, he started taking classes at the girls' school, and there were several of us who were so Americanized that we were thrilled to get the chance to smoke weed any given time or share a bottle of wine, as long as Ace bought it, we never got in trouble. So, we would all meet behind one of the school buildings at lunchtime and smoke up, and Ace always brought the weed.

One day, we were ratted out due to an odor coming from behind one of the buildings that some girls stayed in to finish schoolwork. By the time the teacher came behind the building, that joint had already been put out, but there definitely was a smell. I got into so much trouble I was expelled, even though I denied it and did not have any paraphernalia on me. Amin took the hit for it, but I still got expelled.

April 28, 1975, it was to be for one week.

The road I walked home from school on leaving Ramallah going into El-Bireh.

FRIENDS GIRLS SCHOOL – RAMALLAH

April 28, 1975

TO WHOM IT MAY CONCERN:

Deana Salman is hereby suspended from Friends Girls School for a period of one week from the above date. The reasons are as follows:

1. On Wednesday, April 23, she was absent from school without an excuse and lied persistently about such absence in the face of the school attendance record, the testimony of all her teachers and the personal knowledge of the principal.

2. Since entering the school on February 25, 1975 she has frequently been absent from classes without explanation, even though she was marked present in the homeroom period.

3. On at least one occasion she left the school without permission during the school day and was absent from class.

4. By the testimony of schoolmates she has been involved in the use and pushing of illegal drugs on the school grounds. Although she has not been actually caught in this act, the suspicion is raised by the fact that separate groups of students have made the accusation to the principal and to several teachers.

Shirley Tuttle

Shirley Tuttle, Principal

Of course, this type of news travels fast. My mother, naturally, notified my father, who was still in the United States. Within a matter of days, my mother and Ursula said they would be back later they were going shopping. I thought nothing of it because I was grounded for life again. When they returned, my father was with them. I am not lying when I say I literally wet my pants when I saw him walk through the door, and he had nothing to say to me. Then he **whispered** to my sister, *"Go next door* to your Umptie's house."

From there, he called me into the bedroom. He was sitting on the side of the bed and told me to sit down; he then stood up. He bellowed out, *"You smoke dope?"* I did, but I was not readily going to admit it and told him that they did not find anything on me and even the suspension paper said that no product was found on me. But because so many full-blooded Arab girls were jealous, they had also told Mrs. Tuttle also that I had given them LSD! SERIOUSLY, LSD?

Now, that completely blew my mind, especially after finding out it was Redhot cinnamon gum that my mother had sent from the states 5-months prior that they were referring to. They had never had it before, so they made up wild stories telling how it made them dizzy, burned their mouths, and so forth.

The next thing I knew, my father was just wailing at me, yelling in Arabic. My mother, standing at the door, said, *"Don't hurt yourself. Pick something up!"*

So, probably one of the few times in his life he immediately listened to my mother; he picked up a chair, broke it over me, and then started beating me with the leg of the chair. Finally, Mother had mercy on me and pulled him off me. A doctor ended up being called in due to the severity. Nothing was broken, but I had bruised ribs and bruises anywhere my skin was visible, along with a mild concussion, though that went without saying. After looking back at the paperwork and seeing such a great amount of time passing by in me going back to school, it came to mind that I could not go back due to how I looked. And at that point school was going to be a privilege, so I was not allowed to go. I remember when I was allowed out of the house, I had to walk behind my father with my head down. My father made it clear he would never beat me again (I was elated that he felt sad, or did he?)

He then confirmed with, *"I will kill you next time."*

On June 21, 1975, I was readmitted to school.

Trauma 6 age 13.

Then, yet again, yes, you guessed it, I got in trouble for leaving school grounds with other Arab girls. We snatched a taxi, one of the longer ones; there were 6 of us including Amin (Ace), so more like a smaller limo, then off to *Jerusalem* we went.

Steve Majors, from *The Six Million Dollar Man*, was in town casting for a movie. They said anyone could join in as background extras, so we mingled in and had a blast. We definitely were caught on camera! Whoa! Wait... what did we just do?

Should I publicly admit I skipped school to be an extra in a TV series? Or should I reveal the real reason we went near the *Wailing Wall*—was to get *Hasishah, A compressed form of powdered marijuana. A psychoactive substance that is consumed plain or mixed with tobacco.* I think those of us who went were just so overwhelmed by the trauma of our daily lives that we didn't care at times.

At least we managed to do some '*teenager*' things and create a few memories to hold onto, knowing that the next beating might very well be our last.

Taxi drivers wasted no time reporting to our families. My Aunt Nejah called me into her house since it was right before ours on my way home from school. She already knew I went to Jerusalem, and so did my father!! Ursula took a bottle of ibuprofen to get the family's attention off me, and it worked! She saved my life at that time. Ursula had to be rushed to the hospital to have her stomach pumped, which made the thought of killing me leave my father's head momentarily.

I didn't see my father again until I came back to the States months later.

I stayed with Aunt Nejah for a couple of weeks and wished to continue living with her even after my father left. My mother was cold & hard towards me, so this would be best. Umptie Nejah saved me & Ursula many times from the wrath of Rhoda as well.

Another time, we skipped out to the corner store, and two gals ended up purchasing alcohol. I freaked out. I had no idea that was their intention, and I knew that trip was going to be reported to my family before I even got home, even though I did not partake, I did not want the next beating to send me to my grave, and this time my fathers brother Ummo *Mofeed* would be doing the beating since my father had already left back to the States. Déjà vu from 1967 beatings!

I went home to Umptie's house, I was right, the family was enraged, especially *Mofeed*. My Umptie would not allow him into her home knowing what would come next if she did.

At this point, I was so upset because I knew I was not believed, and I told Umptie *Nejah* that I was willing to give up the girl who bought the alcohol.

Umptie and I set out walking as you do in the smaller realm of El-Bireh, to go to *Maggie's* house. I was ready to be vindicated!! We were welcomed in, my Umptie started to tell the story of me being the only one accused of buying alcohol and that there were 4 or 5 of us in the group, Maggie being one of them who could attest to me not drinking, purchasing, or having anything to do with that whole ordeal, but Maggie totally threw me under the bus. I had asked Maggie before to come clean, and she would not, so I had no choice. I felt terrible; Maggie was severely beaten and never did come back to school.

The last I heard before leaving back to the States was that her family married her off. That was the last I ever heard of or about Maggie. Her sister, *Cairo*, would not even look at me, let alone let me know how Maggie was doing. I tried one last time before leaving, but it was a no go!

Just a few months after that, my mother was having a conflict with my Ummo *Mofeed*. He was a real ass and troublemaker, always trying to stir things up. He did not like that my sister was close with one of our first cousins, *Nabaih*, and insisted, saying, *"They should marry if they were going to be seen together in public."*

My mother had just enough of him and his mouth and told us girls we were going home. I can remember my mother going to the travel agent to book our flights. You must give a 72-hour notice for departure, especially if only the woman is leaving the country with kids and her being a solid Non-Islamic American.

Mother did everything right and got us out of there; she, too, had enough of living up to my father's name… to include the wrath of his family members, including *"the other"* sister-in-law, who was a greedy self-centered woman. I was thankful mother allowed me to return home as well. *America-bound!!!!*

Teenage life was in its prime. Going to school, working after school, and working weekends in the stores. My father would drop my sister at one store and me at another every Saturday morning. This particular Saturday, it was the first of the month, check cashing day, along with most in the area receiving food stamps that my father would pay cash .50 cents on the $1 for them. Like any other Saturday, safe keys in one pocket, a bundle of cash in the other in order to *"make the deals"* under the table so to speak.

I was on the phone with Ted's wife, Sheila. Ted was our butcher; my father had bought the store from him and his wife with the condition he stays on as butcher for a few months until we got the store settled *Fateeh's* way. So, I am on the phone, and Alex, the stock boy, was there doing his Saturday job, my back to the door, leaning on the counter. I felt someone poking me. I turned around, ready to bite whoever's head off, usually expecting some kid wanting two pieces of *Bazooka* bubble gum. NOT THIS TIME!!

There it was… A pistol pointed right in my face!! I was instructed to hang up the phone, instead I set the phone down on the counter, hoping that Sheila would hear some of what was taking place. I was told to head to the back of the store. Upon doing that, our stock boy, who had already begun stocking the shelves, was snatched also, and told to walk to the back of the store with his hands up. Naturally, we both complied. When getting to the back and going behind the meat counter, *Ted* looked up with fear on his face and disbelief and cried out, *"Oh my God, we're getting robbed!"* With that being said, one of the two robbers got extremely nervous and began to bark orders at Ted. Then the unthinkable happened: the gun went off, shooting Ted in the face.

The two men turned and fled as quickly as they could. The stock boy Alex went to help Ted as I went to call 911. To my surprise, Sheila was still on the phone; I told her we needed to hang up and that I needed to use the phone. She could tell by my voice something was extremely wrong, so I told her we had just been robbed. She questioned about Ted, and all I could mutter was, *"I need to go. I need to call for help."* at that time, I believe she knew we were in serious trouble, and she hung up just before saying she was on her way.

I called 911 and then immediately went to try and help Ted. Alex was sitting on the floor, holding Ted's head in his lap with rags wrapped around his face, blood all over him, as well as Ted and the floor. Before the ambulance got there, Ted opened his eyes, giving a look that will haunt me forever. I could see the fear in his eyes that he could be dying. The police came, the ambulance arrived and Ted was rushed to the hospital.

After my father arrived, and questions being answered, we took off for the hospital as well. This is where I know God is so incredibly good. Ted pulled through surgery, leaving a fragment of the bullet lodged in the bottom of his skull, with doctors saying that the only thing that saved him was his bottom dentures; when the bullet hit his face in the chin area, his dentures shattered, which caused the bullet to lodge downward. Ted eventually made a full recovery and retired.

My father felt it was OK to take me back to the store and finish working that day. Typical Arab thinking. So, as I was instructed to do so, that is exactly what I did, however, the store was chaotic with investigators eventually having to close the store for the rest of the day.

The following Saturday, an elderly gentleman came into the store named Adam. He was a regular and always came in and bought his fifth of *Thunderbird* whiskey and cashed in his food stamps on Saturdays. Adam asked me what had happened, and I gave him a brief scenario and told him that Ted was going to pull through.

He was happy to hear that, and then he said, *"Were they black?"* I replied, *"Yes, Adam, they were."*

He was sad to hear that; most everyone knew everyone in the neighborhood, and he said there had been reports of two young black men robbing several businesses in the area lately. Sadly, come to find out, one of the young men was his son, *Sonny*. Adam made it a point to come into the store and apologize profusely for his son's actions. My heart went out to Adam; he was a good man and a gentle soul. I never saw Adam again as my father received much grief from my uncle CK, my mother 's brother, who insisted that the store was no place for a 15-year-old *white* girl. **Trauma 7 age 15**

Chapter Six

MISCAL AND THE ENGAGEMENT

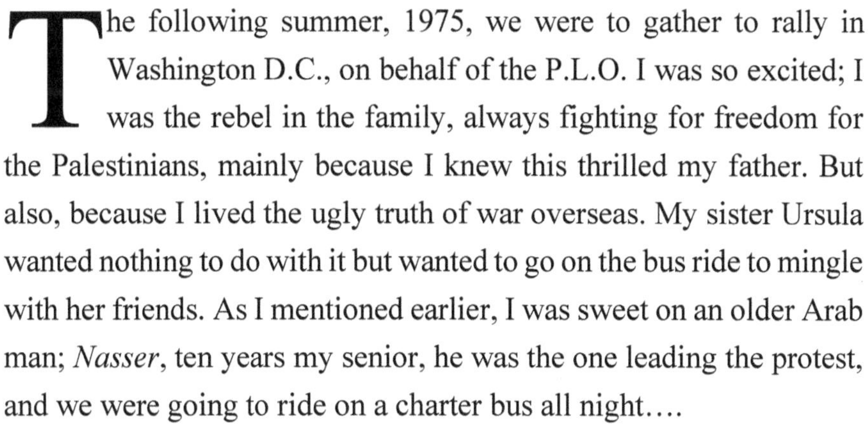

The following summer, 1975, we were to gather to rally in Washington D.C., on behalf of the P.L.O. I was so excited; I was the rebel in the family, always fighting for freedom for the Palestinians, mainly because I knew this thrilled my father. But also, because I lived the ugly truth of war overseas. My sister Ursula wanted nothing to do with it but wanted to go on the bus ride to mingle with her friends. As I mentioned earlier, I was sweet on an older Arab man; *Nasser*, ten years my senior, he was the one leading the protest, and we were going to ride on a charter bus all night….

I could not wait!!! It was a dream trip!!"

Nasser told me years later, after I found him on social media, that he and his family had left Youngstown. It was never the same after *Fateeh,* **"Big Al,"** known in the Arab Community as the *godfather* from *El Dar Toweel,* **"The Big House,"** had passed away.

The rally was canceled, and I was both upset and angry. I loved being a rebel and would attend any event I could, even though, to this day, I am still unsure about what exactly I was protesting—other than being told, ***"We are a people without a home due to the Israelis!"***

Yabbah (Father, Dad) desperately wanted to make it up to me since I became an Arab rebel to include writing and printing in the *Youngstown Vindicator* an article on Palestine, and he said, *"I'll send you anywhere you want to go."* I was so longing for his love yet once again. Well, that did it for me...I wanted to go to Oakland, California, to visit with Dora, whom I desperately missed from overseas. She now lived with her father, *Suleiman*, and his second wife, two small children and *Miscal*. I do not remember her sister Fatima being around, but I knew she had married, so I am assuming she moved to wherever he was living in the States, and that's how Dora came to live back at her father's tiny 2-bedroom apartment.

Off I went to Oakland for three glorious weeks!!

I do not remember the entirety of the trip other than a few blotches of vivid images - snippets of conversation, the occasional laughter, and fleeting moments of scenery.

However, I met her brother *Miscal* there, whom I thought was charming and not bad in the looks department. He was tall, with dark, Afro-style hair and dark chocolate eyes that I saw nothing but stars in. Did I mention he had amazing build on him? Well, he sure did; he worked out every day and was on a *Rocky Balboa* kick as half the world was, including drinking raw eggs every day, jogging uphill, and then doing the victory dance. He was amazing… but wait, there is more!

He was kind to me, and I spent time together with him in the small grocery store his father owned. He was in his last year of high school, Dora was in her junior year, and I had just completed my freshman year in Youngstown, Ohio, at Ursuline High School, a private Catholic school. Our time together was wonderful; we could not get enough of each other. Picnics and visits to the park became our favorite activities.

However, Dora was always with us because Arab girls do not roll solo with any male without a chaperone. We were all fine with that. *Miscal* & Dora knew what a 1/2-breed was like. In America, you are an Arab, and in Palestine, you are *Amrikie* (American).

So, needless to say, we knew what time it was when it came to following the rules. Well, let us say we did the best teenagers could do. I was over the moon when he gave me his high school ring and sharing that first kiss felt like a dream come true, filled with stars and butterflies. I took it as a sign that we were officially together. We had already spent hours on the phone, with Dora either connecting us or me calling for her and him jumping on the line. By the time I flew back home, about a 4-hour flight, Miscal's father, Suleiman, had already called my father, putting the bug in his ear for marriage.

The Engagement

In the winter of 1975, at *The Greek House* Restaurant in *Lake Milton, Ohio*, Miscal & I was engaged. My father reserved the entire restaurant for the evening. The *Hafla* (party) was tremendous as people from all over the country came. I had never seen my father so happy. He was bursting with pride… Over ME!! Or was it because he finally was on his way to proving I was worthy of an arranged Arab marriage soon to follow? Regardless, the $5000 spent on the party

(Mother sent me the receipt like 30 years later) was worth every penny to him, as well as me believing I finally had what I had been longing for – *a perfect Arab child of Fateeh's!!!!*

Miscal and I would come to visit each other every few months, not to mention the hours of talking on the phone. But then, with one of his visits to Ohio while in *Perkins*, pancake house on Belmont Avenue, we were having a great talk about our future together, and I told Miscal about my school plans. I was planning to finish high school early because I skipped a grade due to taking all credit classes and going to summer school, which was coming up again. I wanted to move right into college for my psychology degree.

However, Miscal replied, *"No more school!"*

I was in shock. This was not the guy I fell in love with. Something had changed in him. I remember asking why we were even getting married if we did not want to make something of our lives instead of working for our parents in their grocery stores and one day getting our own store, which was not my idea of a great life.

He then **whispered**, *"You are Fateeh's daughter; that is why I am marrying you."*

Yes, the bitter truth came out: although he did like me, this was clearly an arranged marriage. Arranged marriages are made from respect, my Aunt Nejah once told me, and love comes later. I was crushed learning it was because of my father's name and not the person I was.

Mr. Popovich, a short, stocky, serious Italian psychology teacher and my mentor, was so true in everything he had said to me over the past year. He would always end our conversations with, *"This is NOT normal, 15-year-olds do not get married off in this country; this is not our (American) culture, and even in other cultures, this is wrong."*

Mr. P was always so loving and caring in all the words he chose, and he encouraged me to wait along with everyone on my mother's side of the family. But hey, I had a carat diamond on my finger, my father's love, and my mother's, I thought.

"Thank God she is not my problem any longer." I overheard mom **whisper**! So, she thought!! The backfire started!!!

Summer school started, and I was noticed by a guy named *Ralph Jr*. He was from a blue-collar family. His father owned a painting company, and Ralph Jr was already a well-groomed painter at the age of 17. He was about 5'10, with sandy blonde hair to his shoulders, balding on top at such an early age. He and I ended up meeting a couple of times in the gymnasium during summer school. ***OH BOY, now, I was in love, for real this time!! For sure, this time!!*** He was a mover and a shaker. He was a druggie, but that really did not matter, as I thought, and he was cool. Also, he did not know who my father even was…. **BONUS!!!** Unfortunately, his father knew of my father and once said to me, *"Don't let your ol' man dictate your life to you."*

Ralph's mother, *Barb*, loved me, and I liked her well enough. She was lonely and lived vicariously through *"Ralphie."* Sometimes a bit nosey, and I often wondered how involved she would be if I ended up being with my true prince, HER Ralphie.

Never could I have made up what came next!!!

Chapter Seven

VIOLATED

Miscal knew something was up on what was to be my last visit as *Deana Elaine Fateeh Abdul Salman* to his home (family apartment). Oakland, California. I did tell his sister Dora, that I was falling for another guy. Why I did that, I will never know!! Young and dumb, that should have been the last person I confided in. But we were besties!!!

We all decided to go to the park to hang out and smoke a joint, as we usually did. Always having a fun time. I thought nothing different in this visit to the park. I just had to work out some crazy thoughts in my head. Miscal & I, before I knew it, were alone. Where had Dora gone? He started kissing me, which I was no longer comfortable with. We sat on the side of the hill where no one could see us sitting in a patchy forest part of the park.

The next thing I knew, Miscal said that he had spoken to my father about this *"other guy"* that I had told Dora about and did not want me anymore because I was not pure any longer. He said my father was furious and told him he could…

"Have me to prove I was a virgin." No way was Miscal going to

let his prize go; I am positive he and Dora orchestrated this next event.

I was violated!! I tried yelling, muttering, *"Stop, my father will have you killed!!!"*

He said, *"Shut the F&%$ up; he already knows what I am doing...then* **whispering***...this is by his order."*

I was limp, no more fighting, and my virginity, as well as part of my soul, was lost forever. Where is my God? Blood was running down the hill into a stream from the plush grass we were on; looking upward behind me, I saw just a glimpse of Dora. There was her brother's partner, keepin' watch. I had been so violated and betrayed in so many ways. I wanted to die!!!

Trauma 8 age 15

Now understand, this is not something you tell your father that happened, but definitely, something used for blackmail (from Dora and or Miscal) if I did not marry Miscal. Dora was furious with me that I was rejecting her brother, and I was too young and dumb to realize what I had confided in her should have never happened. Finally, time to go home. I returned broken, sad, mad & filled with hatred for so many people at my young stage of life.

Definitely hated my mother for not caring about the event at Perkins Pancake House. I told her the whole story; she could have cared less.

Oddly enough, she said, *"Does it have anything to do with that new guy from summer school?"*

Now, how did she know that? Well, I told Dora, and Dora told

Miscal & his sister Fatima. Fatima and my mother just loved each other and stayed in contact. Fatima confided in my mother about Ralph. Mom always felt a special something for Fatima & her siblings due to their mother dying from cancer and her caring for siblings until their father remarried a woman half his age to make more babies. Her father could get redemption for himself and go with an Arab wife now since he went Brazilian the first go around.

So here we go, the mindset of a hillbilly hill-raised woman, working hard also for her lifestyle, the one that she especially wanted to continue living. This information would crush my father, and the humility in the Arab community would cause an early death for me.

One day, Mom told me she was taking me to a Dr to test my virginity. What? Why? I had no choice but to tell my mother what happened in California. She, of all people, would understand at least the rape part. I know in my heart mom had also been abused for years by many, including my father. She asked Dora, and naturally, she would deny it. Mom, however, did believe I was not a virgin and thought Ralph was the culprit, and that is why I did not want to marry Miscal, because of the love I felt for Ralph.

I had enough!! I was only 15, everyone that "told me so, TOLD ME SO!!"

Chapter Eight

THE RUNAWAY

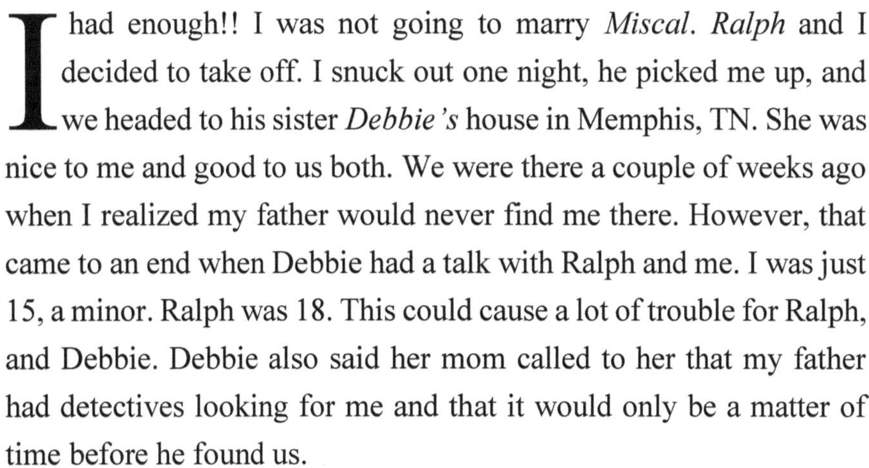

I had enough!! I was not going to marry *Miscal*. *Ralph* and I decided to take off. I snuck out one night, he picked me up, and we headed to his sister *Debbie's* house in Memphis, TN. She was nice to me and good to us both. We were there a couple of weeks ago when I realized my father would never find me there. However, that came to an end when Debbie had a talk with Ralph and me. I was just 15, a minor. Ralph was 18. This could cause a lot of trouble for Ralph, and Debbie. Debbie also said her mom called to her that my father had detectives looking for me and that it would only be a matter of time before he found us.

So, I did what I felt was the right thing, especially since I did not want harm to come to Ralph or his family. We went back to Youngstown; I called the police dept and asked to speak to the detective in charge. When Detective Sparks spoke to me, we came to the agreement that I did not have to go home. I could go to a runaway home but just turn myself in. I was very intentional with him so he would understand how afraid I was for Ralph and myself. He guaranteed my safety.

Ralph dropped me at the police station, where Detective Sparks greeted me. He said he would be informing my family that I had returned, and I would be in a safe house. So far, everything we agreed upon was fair and true to our agreement.

The group home was for runaways who either would not go back to their homes due to abuse or court ordered.

We had school there, chores, and free time, as well as one-on-one counseling. Life was calmly flowing for a second.

One day, I was on the front porch talking to Ralph; he came to visit all the time. This particular day on the porch, I thought I saw a ghost!! My father!! I absolutely knew I was a dead gal walking. I told Ralph to go…RUN…my father would have him killed. I took off and went all the way downstairs into the basement and hid behind the hot water heater scrunched down. It was dark; no one would find me… until they did.

Apparently, the counselor knew my father was coming to talk to me; it had been set up. I do believe the counselor believed me how frightened I was of my father, but he really had no idea what he was capable of.

I agreed to come upstairs and talk to my father, with the counselor present in the room. My father was as sweet as he could be. Academy award performance *(now you know how my performances came about)* and had the counselor convinced that I would be safe at home and no harm would come to me if I went home. Mr Raven, the counselor, did confirm that he and Detective Sparks would randomly be checking in on me. What they did not know is when I finally disappeared, my father would simply say…

"She ran away again."

I would never be found!! No body, no crime. Even at an early age, I knew that!!

I was told I was going to be picked up in two days to go to what they called home. LORD HELP ME! I knew Jesus and accepted him in my heart on April 1st, 1971. Surely, HE would hear my cry this time, or perhaps the single set of footprints were those of HIS carrying me as I look back.

I called Ralph to ask what happened on the porch with my father and to tell him what happened with the counselor. Ralph told me that my father came up to him while he stayed on the porch (Ralph was not going to run from my father; after all, his father was part of *"The Teamsters Union."* We all know what that means...for those who do not...it was an organization back in the days of the 70s & '80s', perhaps even on going, that was called upon to administer a beatdown or, even worse, if certain parties, people, did not comply to *Teamster Rules!!! We all knew there were two sets of Teamsters!* Ralph told me my father came up to him and said, *"I thought I told you to stay away from my daughter,"* as he slipped his hand inside his coat and put it over his side holster. My father loved his 38-snub nose.

Ralph replied after he reached around his jacket and put his hand on his gun tucked in his belt, *"No Sir, you never have told me that because I have never spoken with you."* It started getting a bit heated when the counselor came on the porch to bring my father inside to have our meeting.

After I heard this, I knew Ralph was the man for me. No one ever stood up to Fateeh Salman, AKA "Big Al." My belief, to this day is my father left Ralph alone because even though this was about me, my father respected or perhaps tolerated him for standing his ground.

Moving forward, my father had told the counselor right in front of me that my mother was taking us girls for an end of summer trip before school started to my brother Max's in *Edwardsville, Illinois.* This was just across the river from St Louis. I just figured that my father wanted me out of his sight since I refused to marry Miscal.

The next thing I knew, my mother, myself, Ursula & Dana were on our way to Max & *Katie's,* his then wife. Her sister *Mary* lived there also. We were about the same age. Katie had custody of Mary because she needed to have spine surgery that put her in a full plaster body cast from neck to tailbone for a solid year. She was such a tall, frail gal. After talking with her, she confided in me that her mother was the devil! Ah, at last, common ground!!!

I missed Ralph terribly. I would call him collect when I could get away with it. And at 15, you know love letters were going to be written. I guess I did not hide mine well enough, and my mother found it while we were at Max's. She called me out, and oh my goodness, the fight was on.

All I could hear was. *"You will never see Ralph again; wait until your father hears about this."* Whelp!! That is all it took for me to go psycho…I tried taking it from her, but she was a fighter, no doubt. I grabbed a pair of scissors to stab her with, but we hit the ground rolling.

Honestly, I do not remember how it ended. Either Max came into the house and broke it up, or it was just over when Mom got the scissors away from me. What I do know is that the next day, we were getting ready for dinner, and mom had left after saying she would be back in time for dinner. What she did not say was my father would be joining us. Yes!!! He flew to my brothers...for what? I was not sure unless my father was setting the plot to kill me, as he promised after the 1st and last time, he ever touched me!!!

After dinner, my father asked everyone to leave the house, including Max and his family. My father, mother, and I at the table were left; that is when my father told me if I wanted Ralph, I could have him that he would never man up and marry me. That is when I told my father..." *You are wrong; he will marry me."* We called Ralph's house, his father, my father, Ralph, and myself on the phone.

Ralph Sr. agreed to have me in his home and marry his son. Ralph told my father he wanted us to marry and just leave us be.

My father agreed and said, *"I will have her to you in two days. She is your problem now."* Ralph's family and I were elated.

We left the next morning, thinking I was going to be free very soon. However, on the way to what I thought was going home, we ended up in Chicago, Cook County, Illinois. I asked where we were, and my father replied, *"Miscal's aunt's house, Thea."*

I never could have even imagined or made up what comes next!!!

Chapter Nine

WHERE EVIL BEGAN, CHICAGO

———————⌒●⌒———————

We arrived in Chicago several days later, and as we pulled up in front, all I could think of was the sitcom *All in the Family*. That is what these homes looked like—they were all in a row, with about five concrete steps going up. You could sit on them, a stoop. We went inside and met Thea, Miscal's aunt (his mother's sister). We spent the night, and everything seemed in order. Thea was overly nice to me, which I found VERY strange. I had an uneasy feeling that something was not right.

Sure enough, the next day, my parents announced they were leaving with Ursula and Dana, and I was going to stay there for a while to think about the decision I had made—perhaps even rethink it. My family left me again. My mother, once again, not keeping me safe.

That night, Thea came to me and said she was going to help me. She told me she knew I wanted to be with Ralph, not her nephew. Confessing to me that he neither wants this marriage.

She assured me that if I followed her directions, everything would go well. I went to sleep, hoping that maybe life would become livable.

The next afternoon, Thea said, *"Let's go to your room."* She had me sit on the bed while she drew a hexagon on the floor with white chalk, placing a satanic star in the middle. She then poured gasoline over the lines and set it on fire—right there in the bedroom!

Thea said to me, *"Get up and walk through the fire."*

"No, you're scaring me," I replied.

"If you want to live, follow my instructions," she **whispered**.

I remember walking through the satanic circle several times as she chanted over me in Portuguese. I did not want to do it, but I did not have a choice.

She was so convincing and manipulative; perhaps this was a way out for Miscal and me both. Perhaps she was doing this for the love of her nephew?

After a couple of days, I learned differently. People would come to her door at all hours of the day and night. She would invite them in and take them to her *"prayer room,"* which lasted all of 15 minutes, more or less.

Once, I remember a tall, thin Black woman giving Thea money— $1,500 to be exact. I was peeking through my door as she counted all those $100 bills. After she left, I asked Thea what that was about, and she said people came to her asking her to pray over them, and they paid her for this because she had the power! That is when I had no doubt that she was evil and that I was in big trouble somehow. She always said she did this in the name of Jesus Christ, but clearly, that was a lie. Where was my God? How much had my father paid her?

The next day, she took me to her doctor, saying to me it was time to have a check-up. I had no idea why I needed a check-up. A man dressed in a white, intricately embroidered gown, wearing a hat to cover his head, as some do when praying. His assistant drew blood and handed me a gown to put on. *"The Doctor"* instructed me next to lie on a stainless-steel table that stood higher up in the room, using a step stool to get on the table, then lying on my back.

Okay, not normal!

The ceremony, or *"doctor visit,"* began. He stood at one end, and Thea was at the other end of the table. He had three metal balls about the size of golf balls, which he laid over my stomach and rolled around, up, and down, back, and forth, while seemingly chanting over me. The next thing I knew, I was taken into a medical examination room. I was laid down, legs put into stirrups, with a sheet covering me.

The assistant said to me, *"This won't take long; we are giving you something to make you more comfortable."*

"Comfortable for whatttt…" I faded off.

Once I awoke, Thea was by my side. She told me that I had been pregnant, but it was okay; IT was taken care of, and that I could never let my family know I was pregnant by Ralph! What?? I most certainly was not! I told her I never slept with him. The only time I had intercorse was when Miscal raped me! So clearly if I was pregnant, which they said I was, it was Miscal's.

Years later, I finally realized that they did that because they could not allow me to give birth to Miscal's child; that would have proven my story was true. He had raped me! The timeline would have been there as proof. My father would surely know when that child came out that it was an Arab. So that was Thea protecting her nephew.

I remember lying there, my legs in stirrups, feeling such pain inside, tears running down my face, trying to figure out how this ever happened and why my family left me there. Most importantly… where was MY GOD? Nowhere! HE, too, had left me, clearly because I wasn't a godly child and was just a teenager; I was not important enough for HIM. Where was my Momma? **Trauma 9 age 15**

By the time we got home from the doctor, Thea told me to go lie down and sleep. The next thing I knew, my father was waking me up. I could hardly believe my eyes. He **whispered**, *"Yabbah, everything's gonna be okay,"* he handed me 2 aspirin, and I faded back to sleep.

Later, when I was fully awake, he asked me to go outside with him, and we sat on the stoop in front of the house. He told me everything would be all right and not to worry and that he understood everyone makes mistakes. I tried to tell him that Thea was evil, satanic, and worshipped the devil. Of course, he didn't believe me. That's when it hit me—Thea had already contacted my father and told him I was pregnant. She must have said we could not bring shame to the family because of my having sex with another man. She also told him that Miscal was still willing to marry me to save my father's good name. No kidding, Miscal, really?!!!!!

My father looked me straight in the eyes and said, *"You will marry Miscal."* Then, **whispering**, *"if you refuse, they will find you floating facedown in the river while I am at a party in Washington."* I could not believe my own father was telling me this. I knew it was true though, due to a friend of mine, *Sabah*, whom I knew from overseas, had been forced to marry, and when she came to the United States, she disappeared. As far as I knew, she had left her husband and gone into hiding.

My father then told me the truth about her. He asked, *"Do you remember when Sabah came to the United States with her husband?"*

"Yes," I said. *"I remember they were married overseas when I was there, and then several months later, they left to start a new life in America."*

He proceeded to tell me what really happened to her. She had become such an embarrassment to the family because she left her husband that her father and brother tracked her down in the U.S. and threw her onto the subway train tracks in New York City. Naturally, it was listed as a suicide. I was devastated. I believed my father when he said they would find me floating face down a river! ***Trauma 9 age 15***

The Nikah

To my surprise, the next day, Miscal and his father, Suleiman, showed up at Thea's house. My father was there, and he said, *"We're going to the courthouse to get you married."* The next thing I knew, we were at the courthouse in Cook County, Illinois, sitting in the judge's chambers. My father was called out of the room. Apparently, I was too young to be married in Illinois, even with a parent's signature, because I was not pregnant. Hummm!!! At that time, marriage under 16 was only allowed if a parent signed off *and* the female was pregnant.

Wow, what a relief. I was so grateful that this was not going to happen and that there was nothing my father could do about it. Boy, was I wrong? I had clearly underestimated the power of *Fateeh*.

There I was, standing in front of the judge with Miscal. The *Nikah*, which, in Islamic law, *"the marriage contract"* began. After it was over, the judge looked at me and asked, *"Can you tell me where Mrs. Abdullah is?"*

"My response was, *"His mother passed away years ago."*

The judge chuckled and said, *"No, my dear, you are now Mrs. Abdullah."*

I was in shock. Did this really just happen? Is this legit? How could this have even happened?

When the judge came to the part, *"Does anyone here object to this marriage?"* I turned around and looked at my father and saw a tear, ever so slightly running down his face.

Are you kidding me? How dare you!! Are you really going to make me do this just to save your name? Yes, he was. And come to find out, he paid the judge $400 in cash to look the other way and marry us.

The Walima

The next thing I knew, we were on a plane headed for Youngstown, Ohio—all of us. In Arab tradition, the marriage is a private thing. The reception is what the Arabs look at as the actual marriage, also known as the *Walima*, which means *"feast."*

I was now in the FAWN stage. I was frozen, completely. Now, I would morph into the situation. This was my survival mode, more than I ever realized.

A lot of the next week or so was a blur as the *Walima* was being prepared. My father invited people from all sorts of social classes. Tradition says the groom's family pays for everything. Not this time. *Big Al* was ready to show out, to the tune of $20,000 for the wedding.

Back in the 70's, 20k was a LOT of money. My mother stood right next to him, with her family begging her not to do this. They all thought she had lost her mind again (keyword: *again*).

The Nickell Siblings.

Some of my father's best friends were Jewish and business partners. How crazy is that? There was my father, as two-faced as could be—someone who would send uniforms and cash underground to the P.L.O. to help wipe out the Israelis, yet his business partners were Jewish because they were savvy.

Naturally, very few members of the *Nickell* side of the family were there. My Uncle CK and cousin DJ showed up, but no one on my mother's side could understand what had happened to her brain. Mothers do not do this—they protect and take care of their children. Why would she agree with him? Was it her status as his wife? Was it all his money? Did she fear his wrath? Did she hate me so much that she could not stand up for her last-born child? Was he even my father?

How could I not have all these questions running through my head? What did my father have over my mother's head to get her to go along with this when she, in the past, would continuously argue with him over only God knows what!? Oh, and still, no God to help me. I am not sure what I was expecting from God...perhaps the heavens to open and a white horse appear…?

All I had to do was give my *Nickell* family the word that I wanted to leave. Oh, how I wanted to do that, but I knew it would not turn out well. I could not put that on my uncle CK and cousin DJ, who had always been my heroes. And I could not let Ralph get nailed for murder, as he was in the parking lot waiting for the *"go"* sign. I could not turn this into literally a shotgun wedding.

The night dragged on as the *Walima* continued. Two bands—one American and one Arab. Lambs killed and sacrificed…

"The Halal Way," Halal: when an animal is slaughtered in a manner known as Dhabiha; cutting through the juggler vein, carotid artery, and windpipe in order to drain all blood from the carcass. In Islam, the consumption of blood is considered *Haram*; Forbidden, or

unlawful.

The most upscale foods provided, an open bar. Even I took advantage of that. I felt like I was in a movie. September 6th, 1976. Gifts were given, mostly in cash.

Trauma 10 age 15

The next day, we were put on a flight to Oakland, California, with Miscal's father. We arrived at around one in the morning, and by 7 a.m., they had me up and dressed, ready to go to work in what was now a larger grocery store that Miscal's father owned. I had been to their store many times the previous year, and his father was not wealthy. Clearly, my father had bought this family a new grocery store and made a deal with them to make amends for any embarrassment I had caused.

I found out later that we received about $5,000 in cash and gifts, and Miscal was supposed to use the money for us to continue furnishing our downstairs apartment. He told my father everything was all set and brand new. Liar!!!

We lived in the upstairs apartment with his father, stepmother, and their two small children under the age of two in a two-bedroom apartment. Dora, Miscal's sister stayed in Youngstown and agreed on a marriage there willfully, her husband Mohammad was a good man Every day, I worked behind the register. An employee named Jerome, who stocked the shelves, became my friend. He was a teenage black kid, just trying to earn money for his family and continue with school.

One day, after hearing bits of my story, Jerome came to me with concern written all over his face. He pulled out a joint and said, *"You could probably use this."* I was shocked but grateful. I could fade away and not have to deal with reality…I was told my mother was calling that day to talk to me.

I spoke with mother, telling her that the apartment was a lie; her response was, *"You must sleep with your husband; it is your "duty as a wife"!* MY DUTY??? Apparently, reports had been ongoing of my behavior towards my husband. I asked to talk to my father because I wanted him to know what was going on, how they had lied to him about where we were living, what was done with the money, and how I was being treated.

Her reply chilled me. *"You cannot speak to him. He is in the hospital. He has had a heart attack."*

I knew then that whatever was going to be done, I had to do it on my own.

A few days later, we were invited to Miscal's uncle *Bassim's* house for dinner in *Berkeley, California.* It was the night before my 16th birthday, so it would have been September 25th, 1976. This man was cruel. I had heard stories about him—he was no one to mess with. He was the type who would do the dirty work for anyone who asked.

A Teamster…No, he was the *Arab Mafea.* Worse!

After dinner, he took me into a bedroom, closed the door, and, with a smile on his face, said, *"You have been married several weeks now, and you are not sleeping with my nephew as a wife should. Let me be very clear, my dear, "* as he continued smiling.

"You will never go to school, so get that out of your mind. Your job is to make a family with my nephew. Therefore, if you are not

pregnant within 30 days, then **whispering**, *I will kill you. Do you understand me?"* **Trauma 11 age 15**

I replied, *"Yes, I understand."* I agreed that things would be different, but in my mind, I thought, I cannot do this, I will not do this. I would rather die free than die in restraints, forced into something I was not willing to do. That evening, after we got home, I told Miscal I needed a shower and that I would come to bed soon. He went to bed, and I went out onto the back porch. I smoked a cigarette, even though I had been hiding them. I didn't care anymore. When I went back inside, I was happy to find Miscal already asleep.

That was when I sprang into action, with no plan other than to run. I grabbed a pillowcase, stuffed a few things inside, and took a sheet into the bathroom, where I started running bathwater. I opened the window and lowered my sack to the ground. Then, I turned on the shower and plugged up the bathtub, just to be mean. I went into the kitchen, grabbed some lipstick, and wrote on the refrigerator, **"Thanks for everything. I am out!"**

With the little cash I had snatched daily from the registers and a pillowcase holding all my worldly possessions waiting on the ground floor, I carefully opened the back door and climbed down the fire escape.

This was the last day of my 15th year of life.

Trauma 12 age 15

I no longer will continue to count Traumatic events in my life, I will just play the "Game of Life." I was already so tired at the early age of 15.

Deana Elaine

Chapter Ten

ON THE RUN

Sweet 16

Sweet 16 and on the run from a horrible, arranged marriage, my father, and anyone else he might send after me. I took a bus from Oakland to San Francisco, about ten miles away. Once I got off the bus, I felt a wave of uncertainty wash over me. I was wary of contacting any family members; I didn't know who to trust and wanted to avoid putting anyone in danger over this developing situation.

The subway seemed like the place to go back then. It was chaotic, filled with homeless people, beggars, and what I would call "hippies"—my kind of crew! Simple folks were playing music, dancing, and passing around their hats and guitar cases for tips, living day by day. I quickly became friends with a guy named Chris. He had long hair, bell-bottom blue jeans and played the guitar for tips. I was probably drawn to him because music had always run in my family; anyone who could play on the street and carry a tune had a piece of my heart. I hung out with Chris for a couple of days, surviving on the little cash I had managed to snatch here and there from the store.

On the second day, I realized this was not the life I had dreamt of, and I needed to move on. My gut told me that heading northeast felt right. I managed to hitchhike to Salt Lake City, Utah, and then I called Annie. You remember her? She and Mahmoody had been living in Chicago. Mahmoody was still a real jerk. Even after he and Annie got back together, he was still awful to her. He had tried to kiss me a couple of times when I was just twelve or thirteen. I had warned him that if he did not stop, I would tell my sister, which put a temporary halt to his advances.

You really must know Annie to understand her. She was one crazy gal, now fluent in Arabic, and everyone was afraid of her, Except my father, of course. You did not want to mess with Annie. She insisted I come to her and get off the streets. I hesitated to tell her where I was, but ultimately, I felt I could trust her to protect me, so I decided to head back to Chicago.

Back in those days, hitchhiking was the way to travel. For the most part, you did not have to worry too much about being harmed, even as a teenage girl on the road. Looking back, I must say, that God had favor on me during that time. I should have trusted HIM more.

My instincts told me to find a truck stop, looking back, I realize that was not just instinct—it was the Holy Spirit guiding me. I ended up in a truck stop there in SLC. Those places could be amazing back then; truckers had a code.

After being there for a couple of hours, an elderly waitress named Geraldine (Gerri) took an interest in me. She seemed to sense that I was a girl in trouble, and we talked. I didn't reveal everything, but I shared that I was trying to reach my sister in Chicago. Gerri knew most of the drivers that came through the café and offered to help me find a safe ride.

She went up to the cashier and let her know that I needed a ride headed east to Chicago, asking her to inform me when a driver traveling that route came in. Within no time, a driver named *Paul* sat down at the counter for lunch. I saw Gerri talking to him, and before long, he approached me, introducing himself. He understood my situation and was willing to help. We chatted while he ate, and I could feel he wanted me to be comfortable riding with him.

Before I knew it, I was in a big semi-truck headed to Chicago. It was a pleasant trip—Paul was a true gentleman. We talked about our lives, where he had been, and where he was going. When we finally arrived at a truck stop in Chicago, he wished me well and asked if I needed any money. I declined, thanking him for his kindness, and told him I would call my sister to pick me up.

When Annie arrived, we both cried. She yelled at me, which I had expected, and I took it gracefully. After she vented, she admitted that she didn't blame me. *"The Arabs are crazy, especially our father,"* she said.

The next day, after she opened the grocery store and took care of a few things, she suggested we go to the carnival for some fun. We had a blast riding a few rides—especially the Tilt-A-Whirl, which became our favorite. I won a massive stuffed animal shooting darts; it was huge, nearly three feet tall!

Little did I know that bear would become my friend for many years to come.

One night, while sleeping on the couch, Mahmoody, Annie's husband attempted to molest me. Annie had earlier threatened him with his life if he called my father to tell him I was there, so apparently, he thought he would try to finish what he started years earlier with me.

My screams echoed through the living room, and Annie came flying in, yanking him off me and beating him fiercely. At that moment, I knew I could not stay there any longer.

The next morning, I told Annie I had to leave. She broke down, saying it was probably a good idea, then confessed that she had called our father that morning after the fiasco in the living room. Anger surged through me as I realized he would be driving from Youngstown to get me. I understood then that if he were on his way, I would never see the light of day again if I didn't leave.

Annie could not risk her husband hurting me, and if our father ever found out about Mahmoody's attempt on me or that she had been hiding me, he would undoubtedly deal with both of them as well. But she, too, was still deathly afraid of our father, even though she was married and living her own life.

As time passed, Annie, her husband, and his brother, *Sami*, fled to Palestine, evading the FBI. They had quite the scam going with their grocery store. Back in those days, food stamps were paper that looked like Monopoly money but in regular size. They would pay customers fifty cents on the dollar in cash. Sound familiar?

Sami began stealing first-of-the-month checks, and Annie would sign and cash them through the store. Once they got caught a couple of years later, they wasted no time booking tickets to return home, where Annie and Mahmoody raised their other children in Palestine.

Dana now had three full-blooded siblings.

Before I left, Annie and I had some revealing conversations about our father and my mother. She told me some things I remembered but did not understand until then, particularly about how my mother was so mean to her. My mother treated Annie differently than she did Ursula or me, especially after Dana was born. Annie filled me in on my mother's dirty little secrets. Mom used to skip out of The Hub Club with "a friend" or sometimes two, and Annie would often join them. It was interesting, and I had no reason to doubt her.

Annie did not blame me for running away when she heard about it both times. She confided in me that my father was sending money overseas, saying he wanted to leave Rhoda for a good Arab wife. Annie then revealed something shocking: *my mother did not want me.* It was not that she did not want Deana; she did not want another child after the difficult labor with Ursula.

Apparently, my father had started pricking holes in the condoms; he was a slick one, no doubt. She was livid when she found out she was pregnant with me, especially after my father told her what he had done. Perhaps she was enraged, wondering if I was Fateeh's child.

Mom tried to self-abort using Quinine, but that was an epic fail, she then threw herself down a flight of stairs, hoping it would work. Side bar, recently, I found out at age 63 that I am allergic to Quinine!

I am coming, Mommy Dearest!

The few things I had gathered went into a backpack, and I grabbed my three-foot teddy bear before sneaking out while Annie was not paying attention. I called her once I was on the road, hitchhiking again, with no idea where I was going. She was upset and scared, fearing my father would beat her, even though she was a grown woman and married. I urged her to call him immediately and tell him not to leave, that I had taken off without her knowing. That might just save her life from his wrath.

At that point, I was not sure what to do or where to go. After wandering the streets for a while, I realized I had to reach out to a solid family member—my Aunt Maddie. When I called her, she said, *"Get yourself to the bus station. I will wire you money for a bus ticket to Toledo. Let me know when you get the money, the ticket, and your arrival time. I promise not to tell your father."*

I believed her; she had always been on my side, especially when I had confided about not wanting to get married during the last summer visit. She and her husband, *Uncle Petrochelli*, an authentic Greek man, picked me up from the bus stop. I will never forget how she laughed as she told the story of how she and Uncle P picked me up, with me clutching a teddy bear bigger than I was, looking like a total wreck.

When I saw my aunt and uncle, everything finally hit me. I broke down right there at the bus stop. Aunt Maddie tenderly picked me up and reassured me that everything would be okay and **whispered,** *"Let's go have fun,"* and off we went to the Greek festival.

To this day, whenever there is a Greek festival, I try to attend; it brings back good memories of being free and surrounded by love and protection.

My life with Aunt Maddie and Uncle P was wonderful. I lived with them in their cozy condominium, where they owned a restaurant and a few diners in Toledo. I was never afraid of challenging work, so I started washing dishes and helping around the house however I could. This blissful period, however, lasted only a few short weeks.

One day, Aunt Maddie sat me down and delivered some troubling news: my mother had called her to say that my father had hired two detectives to find me. I was left wondering whether my aunt had contacted my mother first to let her know I was safe. If she did, I was relieved that my mother had not given me up to my father. Hearing that was surprising, but I knew Aunt Maddie must have played a significant role in it.

According to my mother, two gentlemen in suits had visited my father's grocery store, R & S Market, on Elm Street in Youngstown. Yabbah was speaking with them privately, and eventually, my mother managed to extract the truth from my father. He tried to pass them off as *Campbell Soup* sales associates, but she was not buying it, especially given their attire. It was then that he admitted to hiring detectives to track me down.

Faced with this new reality, Aunt Maddie and I devised a plan for me to go live with my brother Max in Edwardsville, Indiana, where he lived with his wife and her sister. So once again, I found myself packing up, preparing to move yet again— two suitcases, put on a plane.

Max was there to pick me up with his tender heart, arms opened wide.

Chapter Eleven

LIFE WITH MAX & KATIE

━━━━━━━●━━━━━━━

My brother Max was nothing but pure love and understanding, along with his wife, Katie. However, Katie's sister, *Marie*, was a real handful. Katie had been given guardianship of Marie in her teenage years due to their mother's struggles with alcoholism. Marie needed extensive spine surgery because of scoliosis, which meant she would be in a body cast for a year.

In the beginning, we all tried our best to behave. At such young ages, Marie and I were both broken from the trauma of our parents. Max and Katie were incredibly patient with us. I started school that fall at *Edwardsville High School* and quickly made new friends.

Several months passed, and life seemed to be settling down. My two new friends, *Laurie* and *Brenda*, brought excitement into my world. Laurie was the fun, crazy one who would sneak us *Boones Farm* strawberry wine during lunch or right after school, giving our group of "*wannabe*" cool girls a little thrill. Occasionally, someone would manage to bring a joint to smoke. Ah, life was finally falling into place!

Brenda was dating an Afghani man named *Ahmad,* who was in college at the time. She eventually introduced me to one of his friends, *Amjad,* who was also in college. He was such a gentleman. They did not drink or smoke, which helped me clean up my act a bit. Both guys were kind and generous, and they never violated our boundaries.

However, Amjad was in his twenties, and I could not tell my brother about him. So, naturally, I lied whenever we went out. One day, Max and Katie announced they would be going out of town for the weekend and told Marie and me to behave ourselves. What did I do? Exactly what any normal 16-year-old would do… I threw a party! Marie was terrified and completely against it, knowing the wrath that would come from Max and Katie if they found out.

Brenda and Ahmad spent the night, and I let them stay in my brother's bedroom. BIG MISTAKE! When Max and Katie returned, Marie spilled her guts to them, including my *supposed threat* to throw her down the basement stairs and claim I had warned her not to walk on the stairs since she had just gotten out of her brace. What a story, right? She was not wrong!

After I **whispered** through the door, *"I am going to throw you down the stairs"* ... Marie locked herself in the bathroom until they got back from their trip, knowing it would be less than an hour now. As soon as they entered the house, she came flying out of the bathroom, her face swollen and red from crying. I tried my best to explain that she had gotten on my nerves so badly that I had threatened her but never meant it seriously. I denied having anyone sleep over but admitted to the party.

Unfortunately for me, Katie found dark curly hair and a man's sock in their bed. Totally busted! I was grounded for two weeks. Ah, the joys of teenage life!

On the brighter side, Max had gotten my divorce annulled since it had been illegally executed. Life was good!

Laurie was working at *Western Sizzler* at the time, so she could not hang out with us on some nights. This kept her in my brother's good graces. After I regained my freedom and was told NOT to hang out with Brenda, naturally, the first person I called was Brenda.

Brenda and I decided to go for a joyride just to hang out. I told her I would pick her up. Max and Katie were generous enough to let me use the second car since I had gotten my driver's license in Toledo before I had to go into hiding once again from my father.

On this particular day, I felt as if Satan was harshly attacking me. I called myself a Christian, even though I was way in the left lane and running on truly little faith. But on this day, it was almost as if I had no control over my thoughts. My head was swirling, and flashbacks of my past haunted me. Even though my brother was able to get the marriage annulled, that did not erase the trauma. The ***Tragic Whispers*** kept flowing in my head.

I still felt the pain of the past, and anger began to bubble inside me.

As Brenda and me supposedly "*joyfully*" rode around, I spotted a trail in the woods at the park where we often hung out. Before I knew it, I had taken the car down this path, which initially seemed wide enough for a car—until it was not. The path narrowed down to a bike trail, and we were so far in the woods that I could not turn around or even back out. I had no choice but to keep slowly moving forward. I felt myself picking up speed, even though I had no idea what I was doing or why. At one point, Brenda said, *"Girl, what is going on with you? Are you trying to kill us?"*

"I'm not sure," I replied, fear gripping my chest. *"I am scared in my head and hear all these voices. I just want them to go away."*

"Lord, help me," I cried out. Instantaneously, a clearing appeared, and we found ourselves out of the woods, staring at a small, old-time white church complete with a steeple.

I pulled in and said to Brenda, *"We need to go into this church."* She laughed, saying, *"Yeah, better than you trying to kill us on a bike path!"*

In we went. The church reminded me of the one I grew up in, *Bible Baptist Temple* in *Youngstown, Ohio.* There were rows of wooden pews with faded red carpet on the floor, and the pulpit sat right in the center with benches behind it for the choir.

As we walked up the middle aisle, we thought no one was there. Then, from the back came *Pastor Ray.* His face was soft and gentle, silver haired with signs of aging, with a calming voice as he welcomed us to the church. Pastor Ray asked what he could help us with. At that moment, I saw shadows crawling on the walls, and a picture flew across the room.

Brenda nervously blurted out, *"She needs help; she's about to lose her mind, and we were led to this church."* Anger bubbled inside me, and I told Brenda to stay out of it—that I was fine. Pastor Ray said, *"Just talk to me and tell me what you're feeling."*

Reluctantly, I began to share my story about my arranged marriage. I told him how I was placed at my ex-husband's aunt's house before being married off and that she was wicked—a daughter of Satan. As I recounted the evil she inflicted on me, including forcing me to step over a fire lit on top of a pentagram, the church suddenly rumbled, and another picture went flying.

Pastor Ray looked at me intently and said, *"You need to be released from the hold Satan has on you, and the evil that Thea put on you needs to be broken!"*

Pastor Ray went right into prayer over me, laying his hands on my head. By this time, I had fallen to the floor in a fetal position. I remember hearing him say, *"In the name of Jesus, come out, come out; you have no place in this body."* I'm not sure how much time passed, but when I came to, I could tell from Pastor Ray's face that *"all was well in my soul."*

After chatting a bit more and calming down, he said, *"Jesus didn't leave you; He was carrying you."* A peace washed over me like I had never known before. We left.

It felt as if the world had been lifted off my shoulders. But then reality set in. My brother was going to be so angry that I had noticeably scratched the car on both sides. I honestly did not think he would believe the entirety of my story, but I did not want to lie at this point. So, I decided to go with, *"I went down a path that ended up being a bike trail, and in order to get off the trail, we had to see it out."*

I was right; he was upset, and naturally, I was grounded. I took the hit and left it at that. In my head, I did not lie; I just omitted some of the details.

I soon started working at *Western Sizzler* with Laurie to get out of the house since I was grounded and could go nowhere. Laurie had moved out of her parent's house when she turned 18 and was living in a single-wide trailer. I was just 17 at that time, and I started to think, wait a minute—I am 17 and emancipated, and I am getting grounded for a month?! Nope, that was not going to work. So, Laurie offered for me to move in with her, and I did.

School was out; it was summertime. Laurie and I would go to work together, and she got me a second job at Fat Cats, a bar that had once been a slaughterhouse. It was the coolest place ever! It had nine different bars in it, and some of the servers were on roller skates. Different areas had different music playing. Now, this was my dream job! I started as a barback until I learned the ropes of mixing drinks, although they sometimes needed me to just work the beer bars. Fake ID never failed me!

Eventually, Laurie and I were both let go from Western Sizzler (the only job I would ever be fired from in my life), but that just gave us more time to pick up shifts at Fat Cats.

The next thing I knew, a little cocaine started to become available. You can find anything at a bar, especially in the '70s. Max was aware of my changing lifestyle. He was under conviction; he and Katie had started attending Sunday church.

Max then told me he could not ignore the lie he was living any longer and wanted me to move back into his house. Besides, out of love for me, he said if my father found out I was living in Edwardsville with him, it would be better than him finding out I was living in a trailer, working in a bar.

I was so tired of living with the threat of my father finding me. I was ready to face the music—either kill me or let me go. But I was heading back to Toledo, Ohio, the only place I felt safe, with my cousin DJ and my Aunt Maddie.

So, my plan started: I was going to save money like crazy and get out of Edwardsville. However, just days later, Laurie received devastating news about her sister *Beth*. Beth was set to be married in just two months but had been diagnosed with stage four pancreatic cancer. Laurie said she would need to move back home to help care for her and be with the family. This was completely understandable, especially since Beth was her only sibling.

At that time, I had no idea how I was going to leave and get to Toledo. I called Brenda and told her what had just happened. She then mentioned that Amjad had been asking about me and wanted to see me again but did not know where I was. Per my request, Brenda had not told him where I lived or worked. I just did not want to go through the Arab thing all over again, especially since he was getting serious fast. However, this seemed to be a conceivable way out for me, so I contacted him.

We met up a couple of times, and I finally told him I needed help getting out of town, that my father knew where I was, and I could not bear the thought of my brother, or his family being caught up in my father's wrath. To my surprise and immense gratitude, Amjad showed up one day before I moved out of Laurie's with a car. He said he had paid $200 for it and then handed me the title and $25 in cash for gas money. He told me that although he was in love with me, he understood Arab traditions. He agreed I needed to go somewhere safe.

Amjad's love started to restore my faith in the Arab world and helped me realize not all Arabs are of the same beliefs. So, I packed what little I had and said goodbye to Ahmad, Brenda, and Laurie. Big Blue Bear in the back seat., off I went.

I was hours down the road when I knew I needed to call Max to let him know I had left. He was not happy and tried to talk me into coming back, but I just couldn't. We ended our call with *"I love yous."*

For the first time in my life, I felt in control of my life and my decisions. I WAS FREE!!! Now what? An easy question: I was headed to Toledo, where I would be safe.

Eventually, I called Laurie to check on how her sister was doing. Beth had died on what was to be her wedding day and was laid to rest in her wedding dress. I could not even imagine what sadness Laurie and her family were feeling. She was so devastated that she went into seclusion; I never heard from her again.

At that point, I never looked back or communicated with anyone from our group. I was starting fresh AGAIN. But this time, I had the will and desire to live life. I had been relieved of all my demons and was thinking clearly. I was a survivor, ready to face life with some sense of normality. What was I thinking? There was no normality in our family. We were dysfunctional. But at times, we did put the *"fun"* in dysfunctional.

Now, I realize most of my decisions were made from anger and resentment from being put through so much in such a small window of my life.

Chapter Twelve

TOLEDO OHIO-ROUND 2

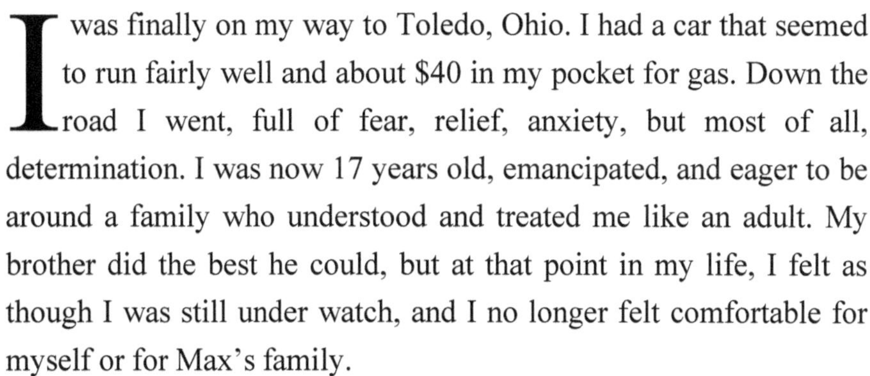

I was finally on my way to Toledo, Ohio. I had a car that seemed to run fairly well and about $40 in my pocket for gas. Down the road I went, full of fear, relief, anxiety, but most of all, determination. I was now 17 years old, emancipated, and eager to be around a family who understood and treated me like an adult. My brother did the best he could, but at that point in my life, I felt as though I was still under watch, and I no longer felt comfortable for myself or for Max's family.

Aunt Maddie and Uncle Petrochelli owned *The Town & Country Restaurant* and were building a small empire on that corner in *Perrysburg, Ohio,* right outside Toledo. Aunt Maddie spoke to my mother, who was in Youngstown, about three hours away. To this day, I am not sure if she spoke to my father as well. But what I was told was that I did not have to worry about my father coming after me or sending *his* people any longer.

Later, I found out that my father finally learned the truth about Miscal and his family, including the wedding money, our lack of a place to call home, and being threatened by Miscal's uncle if I was not pregnant in thirty days. Not to mention, I was put to work in their grocery store less than eight hours after arriving in Oakland, California, from Ohio. I am sure my father was not told of the rape, or he would have undoubtably had Miscal disappear. I was drained—physically, mentally, emotionally, and even spiritually.

Why was my life in shambles? Was I that much of a sinner that I was already paying the consequences of my actions? I was just seventeen. What had I done that was so incredibly wrong or bad that it brought such drama into my life, affecting those around me whom I cared about? I didn't want to see them involved in the wrath of my father. Why, Lord? Why couldn't I just be like normal teenagers, in school, dreaming of my future, asking myself what I wanted to do with my life? Going to dances, football games, and so on?

The past is the past. I am in Perrysburg, Ohio, and life is looking up. My auntie put me to work in her restaurant, *Town & Country*, as a dishwasher. Back then, it was manual dishwashing: scrubbing pots and pans, stacking dishes away, sweeping, mopping—real grunt work. I loved every second of it. Eventually, I moved up the ranks and became an assistant to the head cook. Her name was Lee.

Strange thing about Lee—not sure if it is strange or just unique—she adopted eight children from South Korea, being a single parent to them all. She brought the whole family over, and they all lived with her until they were ready for college. Some of the kids worked in the restaurant occasionally, busing tables or filling in as dishwashers while I was trying to learn how to coordinate the grill, oven, and deep fryers.

Lee was a small lady, smoked two packs of cigarettes a day, drank her whiskey, and at times showed up half drunk to work, only to be escorted out, usually driven home by my aunt. In turn, that gave me the opportunity to advance in the kitchen. She was a crazy badass and definitely a spicy woman. You did not want to cross her in the kitchen. Lee taught me so much about cooking: what to do, what not to do, and how to do it. Looking back now, it was my base for what became a second career down the road some 25+ years later.

Life continued in Perrysburg, Ohio. I was living with my aunt and uncle, working, and went back to high school with encouragement from Aunt Maddie. I only had to go for one semester to get the few credits I needed. So, from September through December, I did it. I completed high school and walked the stage come June of 1979, at only 17 years old.

My teen age moment.

To my surprise, my mother showed up to watch. To this day, I honestly believe it was Aunt Maddie who insisted my mother come. I am not positive, but it is just the gut feeling I had. In the meantime, I had made a fun group of friends, and we liked to go out like any "normal" teenager would want to do. Yes, I felt I was a normal person beginning to settle and make a life for myself.

One night, we "*gals*" wanted to go dancing at this disco club named Disco Blue, just right up the road from the restaurant. Unfortunately, I was not 18 yet, and my Illinois Fake ID was long gone; it had been snatched up by a bartender one night in a bar...somewhere. So, I was unable to join in. But cousin DJ fixed that right up. You see, back then, birth certificates were typed with what seemed to be old typewriters, so DJ changed 1961 to 1960! Solid move! So now I was able to hang with the girls on the weekends.

There were about five of us, sometimes six. It was a blast! We would get a pitcher of beer and share it, meet boys, dance, and never get drunk or stupid. I remember one Friday night; my Aunt Maddie and her friend *Marlene* came to the club to see what we were really up to. They were incognito and stayed in the shadows. Well, I guess they thought we were just too funny.

Aunt Maddie told the story, I bet 50 times over the years, of how we all shared a pitcher of beer between us and thought we were so cool out on the dance floor taking charge. Ha ha! I think we thought we were just that cool as well. My aunt trusted me and had no problem with me going out on weekends as long as I was straight with her.

The time came when help was needed in one of the cafes in

downtown Toledo. DJ owned this one: The Boardwalk. Cousin *Gary Lee,* from Fort Wayne, was around as well, living in Toledo. Early on, we all had that *"Nickell Party Gene"* in us.

Many a time, Gary, DJ, and I would go out together—sometimes separately—and end up at *Frisch's Big Boy* in Perrysburg. That was like a Denny's or Perkins Pancake House back in the day. Gary worked the grill in the café, as did I and DJ when needed.

When you are working in a small countertop café where most seating is at the counter, you get to know your regulars. A bus driver named *Tommy* would always come in after his shift around 11:30 or midnight to have a bite of breakfast and coffee. We became good friends and were sweet on each other.

One night, then DJ came in around 1 a.m., just making the rounds to check on me since I was covering the third shift. Tommy was there. I asked DJ if he would watch the place while Tommy and I took off for a bit. He was fine with it, but he said, *"You know there is no covering for you if Mom shows up."* I was down with that because why in the world would Aunt Maddie come into the café downtown Toledo, 30 minutes from her house, in the middle of the night, right?

Surprise! As I came rolling back in around 3 a.m. to finish my shift… there she sat. Good Lord! I knew I was a dead woman walking. All she said at that time was, *"So glad you decided to join us tonight."* DJ just rolled his eyes like, Cousin, you are in trouble!

Aunt Maddie said, *"I'm leaving now, and I will deal with you in the morning after your shift when you come straight home, little missy!!"* Of all the times I decided to go south, it was with my aunt. I felt horrible. She had been so good to me, and I let her down. I am sure DJ stood up for me and asked her to go easy on me.

The next morning, after getting home, I totally got the *"what for"* from her. Uncle Petrochelli was always so kind and sometimes funny in the way he said things. This day was no different, other than letting me know that I had let them both down. Ugh! I would have rather taken a beating than have that said to me. So now I was grounded for two weeks, nothing but school and home. I was okay with that; to me, that was an easy comply. Although I was emancipated and could leave anytime, out of the respect and love I received from her, I accepted her authority gracefully.

Then I got the big idea to learn how to sew. Yep, I was going to make Aunt Maddie a pair of shorts... yet once again, until the day she passed, it was a story that she talked about the elephant-sized shorts that never got finished. My goodness, I loved her.

Soon after that, I was offered a job at *Corning Glass Co.* It was right across from the restaurant, and we all knew the workers pretty well (sometimes, I would double back as a server when needed). So, I talked to my aunt, and she gave me her blessing—because at 17 years old, it was unheard of to be making $17 an hour? The only catch was that it was a 3rd shift job. That is probably why she was all for it, now that I think about it lol. I worked there for a month or so, saved up money, and traded in the car my friend had bought me in Edwardsville for a Grand Torino. Later, I was sorry I did that—I did not realize what a classic I had. What I really wanted was a Mustang, but I could not afford it with the insurance. So, the salesperson took the cigarette lighter out of the Mustang and put it in the Grand Torino, as a jester of understanding... At times, memories were good.

I had a great income, an excellent job with benefits, and I was safe for the time being. Next on the list was to get my own place. I was thrilled when a couple offered me a flat above their sandwich shop for $100 a month. What a blessing! It was an efficiency top floor and opened out onto the rooftop. Full kitchen and bath, with a sofa couch that pulled out into a bed. It was perfect. I decorated it in a groovy way, and life was good. Blue Bear found his spot on the sofa.

Now that I had been in Ohio for a while, I felt it was safe to reconnect with Ralph. Oh, how I missed him. Naturally, I headed to Youngstown to see my long-lost love. Lawdy, I missed him. We talked all the time on the phone, but that got expensive. Remember, this was the late '70s when you had to pay for long-distance calls.

So, Ralph and I would take turns visiting on the weekends. It was only a 2.5-hour drive—an easy trip. I went there more often than he came to me because of his work as a painter for his father's company, and I knew the "*gang*" there. Eventually, my best friend from high school, *Rita*, started coming with me because she and *Andy* (Ralph's friend) hooked up. Now, the trips were especially fun, and we all stayed at Ralph's parents' house. Momma Barb loved it and loved making breakfast for us all. His father, Ralph Sr., always addressed me with respect, but he and Ralphie (Ralph Jr.) were constantly snapping at each other.

Marry Me Deana

As time went on, our feeling grew more passionate between us.

"Will you marry me, Deana? "Yes, yes, and of course, YES!" Off

to Youngstown, I go: February 15th, 1979, we were married without incident. I was 18.

I dreaded telling my family I was marrying Ralph, not knowing what their reactions would be. Well, that did not go well. Mom was upset, but I brushed it off. Yabba was livid! He said he would "*blow up*" the reception if I went through with it. Well, time to call his bluff. And, in fact, it was a bluff—or Mother talked him down; I am not sure.

Ralph and I were happy for the most. Party favors became a regular thing. Remember, we were hitting the early '80s by this point. Marijuana, Cocaine, Placidyls, LSD, and especially Quaaludes (714's) were all part of life. We frequented a bar called *Lampost*. Ralph still worked for his dad, and we moved, sold, and consumed all the drugs mentioned. Life was great—or so I thought. Well, you cannot live that lifestyle for too long before things start going south. Ralph and I rented a house next door to his parents, and by this time, Barb was all up in our business. I started to dislike her. She seemed to forget that Ralph had a wife now. Our marriage had become a trio.

As that tension grew, we kept working and partying. Then, one morning, my mother and Max (he had come to town to visit, apparently) walked through the front door. It was still open from last night's party. I cannot even begin to describe how many bodies were still there, passed out from a weekend-long party. I was livid that they just walked in. So many people had come and gone that the door was left open, just the screen door closed but not locked. After I got the third degree and was shamed, I asked them both to leave, and they complied.

Life continued, and then the *Lampost Massacre* happened! It was crazy—a bar fight broke out between two different motorcycle gangs. At one point, I had to crack a beer bottle over someone's head. Soon after, I knew it was time for a change. I could not take living next door to Momma Barb any longer and being less than 10 minutes from my parents was not helping either. It was time for the Lampost and the heavy weekend parties to take a break. Perhaps déjà vu from my parent's early years? Who were we becoming?

I found the perfect house out in the country. It was a brick, three-bedroom ranch home with hardwood floors and a basement, complete with a beautiful yard. I even got a poodle, and we named her FiFi: perhaps again, trying to relive the past even with it being completely chaotic and dysfunctional. Life was good. The drug scene had tapered off—few people wanted to make the 30-minute drive out to the country. We were so happy and enjoyed our home. Ralph still liked going out, but I was content for the most staying home. I got a new job at *Yankee Lake Restaurant and Bar* as a server, and it felt like Ralph, and I had a second chance at life.

We had a few more months of good living. Mother even hired Ralph to paint the basement of their house. Somehow, she got my father to agree to it, so at least we had communication, and no one was going to kill anyone!

Eventually, though, I called it quits with Ralph. One day, I walked into our bathroom and saw him sitting on the side of the bathtub, with a light shade of yellow to his skin due to him just shooting up cocaine. That is where I drew the line. I thought he had stopped using drugs, at least the shooting up part, but clearly, I was wrong. I am so thankful

I never got into that mess. Ralph's friend *John* once tried to find a vein in my arm but could not because they were too small. Now, I know that was a Godwink!

As time went on, I moved out of the house Ralph, and I shared. I found a nice two-bedroom apartment on top of *Whacky's Bar* on Belmont Ave. It was right across from the Lampost, where *Mary* worked, which is how she and I became friends. I quickly found a job working at a fast-food restaurant and at The Lampost, too. Life was great, and my father even paid for the divorce—happy to do so, I think, because he thought I would move back into the big house with them. You see, during the time I married Miscal and ran off, fearing for my life, my parents were busy designing and building a brand-new home on *Engleton Ln. in Liberty, Ohio.*

When my father found out where I was living, not to mention where I worked (I was not 21 yet), he threw a huge fit. Luckily for me, the door was steel that led upstairs to the two apartments.

One night, I heard someone yelling my name, *"Deana, Deana, I know you're up there. Shew Hatha?"* (What is this?) He wanted me to come down, and he was so angry. I ignored him. I did peek out from the corner of the bedroom window, and yes, there he was, driving his green well-known Cadillac.

Big Nick, the *OG* I was seeing at the time, said, *"I got this."* He then reached for the pistol he kept strapped to his ankle. I barked, *"Are you crazy? That is my father!"* So, we just waited until he finally gave up and left.

However, the next day, I no longer had a job at the Lampost. I was so angry with my father. Why did he always ruin things for me? I was happy and carefree. Why wasn't he threatening Ursula? Oh, that's right—she gave him a grandson and was one of the well-known *"women of the night"* when it came to the OG legit gangstas to back her up.

Also, there is this…One night, she was out with her married man *"friend"* with reservations to be had at *"The Mansion."* Fine dining at its best. However, when she walked in and was waiting to be seated, there he was!! Our Father, with another woman, drinking, laughing, and seemed to be enjoying his company as well as dinner. Sister immediately **whispered** to her "friend,*" … Let's Go!"* They stopped at a gas station on the way to her apartment, and she called the restaurant, had my father paged, he answered the phone, she **whispered…**" *Are you enjoying your dinner at The Mansion with your "friend?"* "He started stuttering and stammering, lost for words; she then hung up. My father was at her door in less than 20 minutes, trying to explain the *"business dinner"* he was having. So, let us just say that for that reason alone, she became entitled and had her ACE in the hole!

I stayed living in my well-protected apartment (or so I thought) and went to work for one of the *Bashara* brothers at one of their bars on the edge of town. They knew who my father was and felt honored to be able to piss him off by hiring me. Life was good again. Mary even came to work one night a week there. In a noticeably short amount of time, one of the brothers, *Joe,* was found with a plastic bag in his mouth and over his head, left in his car on the edge of town. I no longer had a position there…interesting, right?

Then, one night, Mary went downstairs to sharpen a pencil inside Whacky's. She was an artist, an exceptionally good one, in fact, but we were all still in party mode, so nothing really became of that. She was in her mid-20s, and me pushing 21. We had a lifetime to figure out a career. This one night, Mary did not close the metal door all the way when she came back upstairs. Our friend *Robbie* was there gonna help us paint, wallpaper and drop some window payne (acid).

Mary came back upstairs, opened the door, white as a ghost and **whispered**: *"There is a man outside our door."* We flipped out!! We could see him through the peephole and through the keyhole.

Clearly, this man was not lost. He started knocking while we were watching him, and he had pulled his knife out!! Wholly Crap to the Olah! We were going to die. What a miracle *(Godwink)* it was that he did not snatch Mary when she came up the stairs. We believe he was aiming more for the apartment caddy corner from us that housed an elderly woman. We had no phone and no way of communicating because Mary had painted the windows shut!! Really Mary??? So, we looked out the kitchen window, and there was *Sgt. Dewer* flashing his lights up to our window. That was his call to Mary when he was free to *"fool"* around. We started banging on the windows, yelling for help...well, no one two stories down could hear that.

Dewer and his partner thought we were being funny. Finally, I went and got bright red lipstick and wrote HELP...Backwards so they could read it looking at the window PLEH!! They got it!!! Then came rushing upstairs, struggling with the guy, then arresting him!! Come to find out, he was wanted for rape & robbery! Wow! Did the good Lord have our six that day!!

Mary started getting weird after that. She quit working at the Lampost, started moving Quaaludes dealing with my sister Ursula's baby daddy, and yet one better…she took all the "Lude's "he gave her to sell. When he caught up with her, he told her she had 48 hours to come up with the cash, or he was turning her out to *"work the streets"* until he was paid in full. She came up with the money somehow.

Later, come to find out, my father visited Mary while she was at work one day, on her day shift. He introduced himself and told her that the guy at our door was no accident. Mary vanished. I stayed in the apartment for as long as I could. Mary eventually appeared, apologizing, and telling her story about my father. She moved to the next town over in *Hubbard* and stayed with her parents for a while until she felt it was safe to come out from hiding, since my parents now where in Phoenix for the winter. She felt bad she left me like that and wanted to know if I wanted to try again to be roommate with her that she found a beautiful Victorian house on Elm St. Sure...why not?

It was even better than I could have imagined. Had a big wrap-around porch, vintage architecture, natural wood... and lots of space. So that worked for a while until it did not. We just were better friends than roommates. She stayed, I left, and I rented a room from an elderly lady who had a brownstone.

Now, there we go; I was dating a guy named *Bob*. What a great guy! I really wanted to love him, but I could not. Not my type. He was an *OG* for sure, but again, just not my type. But, oh my goodness, could he show a gal an exciting time. He bought and brought the goods to have a party all the time. Always had an 8ball in his pocket. This was the *"Freebase Era"* of the 80s: A descriptor for the neutral form of an amine commonly used in reference to illicit drugs, most commonly Cocaine.

One of my last memories of Bob, whom we called "*Ferpo*," was he got Mary and me some "*CID*," and she and I took it at my new place, and before I knew it, we were headed to the *Pompanos* with literally 42 stuffed animals in Bob's car in the middle of a crazy ass snowstorm… a 4-hour drive turned into 12. What great days they were back then until they were not. I tried selling cars, serving & a couple of other things, but it was a no-go. I sucked it up and called my parents, who were in Phoenix…there I went, two suitcases in hand, waiting to see what my future held…. Are you starting to see the pattern? I leave!!

Chapter Thirteen

PHOENIX

The beginning of the end for my father

My parents were in Phoenix Az for the winters now, as this became a new trend for them over the last couple of years. My father had somewhat retired for the 3rd time. He had cousins (shocker) in Phoenix and Scottsdale Az who sold gold & silver. They had the rights to the Al-Zuni Indian Tribe Jewelry business to include a gold store as well.

Mom & Dad at Arab Convention in Scottsdale AZ, March 1983.

Back in the day, Indian Jewelry was trending off the charts. My father's cousins had totally tapped into the market at the right time.

A 1-bedroom apartment on the 2nd floor, facing the pool with a beautiful view. I could get used to this life. I slept on the couch.

At only 21, clearly, I had nothing from the past that I would have considered of value. Easy move.

I figure I was there for about a month, taken around and introduced to "the cousins "and their families. I remember lunches out, shopping and just being a free soul with my FATHER's love or perhaps approval would be equivalent, and my mother taking me everywhere she went, and having several memorable mom & me moments I would like to think. I cannot remember all of them other than her taking me to *Fudrukers* for what was the hottest gig going with their burgers, and on another occasion, it was a French café, just she and I still pretending to have normality as mother and daughter.

After enjoying a couple of weeks there, just knowing Phoenix would become my home, my parents told me that my father had to go back to Cleveland Clinic for a small, simple operation, and they would return in 2 weeks.

When he had his open-heart surgery a few years prior, an aneurysm was found on his aorta, less than 5 mm. Until it reaches 5 mm or greater they could not operate on it. So, the time came where it was the right size for removal, and they felt it was imperative to remove it. I wanted to go with them, but my father said *"Yabbah, stay here take care of the home, enjoy yourself, I will be back in 2 weeks."*

The day came for them to leave, we did the love you's, and off they went to Ohio.

April 12th, 1983, the nerves were flying amidst all the family. I spoke with my father before his surgery that day. He was trying to be brave; I knew he wanted it to be over. I told him I loved him, he responded with, *"Yabbah, I love you too."* The normal was never to include the "I "part of I love you, however this time, he did. Staying close to the phone all day, hearing a few updates that consisted of

"No Update, still in surgery." I finally called again that evening, asking about his condition. The nurse said she did not have an update as of yet but would have someone call me. That seemed extremely strange to me. Especially not being able to get through to my mother, Ursula, or my aunt Nejah, who was there, and it being after 8 pm.

I had met a new friend, *Howard*; we bonded like besties in a noticeably brief time. He was from New York, a tall Jewish kid, Gay, and very handsome. I remember him vividly, like yesterday. We always shared a nightcap together…

(an 80's thing to us, a joint, to others as a drink) went to the pool, out dancing, or being mischievous. One time we went to the *Marvin Gaye* concert, dressed to the hilt, out for the night. Marvin Gaye, dressed in a silk purple robe, walked out on stage, lights dimmed; he went sliding across the baby grand piano, singing *"Sexual Healing, "the* crowd went wild….2nd concert I had ever been to. The first had been with Ralph, *"The First World Series of Rock"* in Cleveland Ohio, for 3 days, 2 memorable concerts I will never forget in my early years.

Howard was waiting with me; hours went by, and he had to work the next day; he bounced, but only 2 doors down. Honestly, I wanted to be alone when the call came; the vibes were not good. Sitting, staring at the phone, waiting for it to ring.

What I did not expect was a knock at the door. It was my cousin, *Nasha.* He looked at me and **whispered**, *"It is time to go to Youngstown,"* with tears in his eyes. I knew then it was serious. Nasha instructed me to pack my bag. We were leaving on the next flight. But it was not until we were on the airplane that I had the courage to ask to him, *"Is my father alive?"*

He kept his head down and simply shook his head and **whispered**

"No, he is not." That was the end of the conversation.

I know parenting is hard; I have 5 children & have done it all for, with and to them, but, as a mother, I would never NOT be in contact with my child to tell them or talk to them about their father's passing. Here is one better one, when I arrived at my parent's home, my sister nor my mother did not greet me!! I was a guest, among others.

The Big house (I have never called it home) was my father's pride and joy because he and my mom designed and built it. This was the first time in his life he was able to build exactly what they wanted in the neighborhood they wanted. This house was stunning, complete with a foyer, winding staircase, white carpet, leather furniture, library, grand piano and all the extras. Right out of a movie. Lucy & Ricky.

So many people gather at the house to pay condolences help with food, and arrangements. I do remember, at one point or another, seeing my sisters Ursula and Dana. What is more so remembered is my brother Max arriving the same day at the house (now living in

Dallas) and stepping down the one step into the den, looking at me, tearing up, putting his arms around me and saying, *"Hello Sis, I am so sorry, everything will be all right. "*

Arab Culture, as you would have it, brings female siblings or closest family members to wash, dress & bless appropriately as a *Sheik,* given the father's status and influence globally. He was laid to face the east for the sunrise.

I needed to see my father before this ritual took place. Afterward, you are not to touch him; he was considered Holy and ready to meet Allah. However, my dad was going to heaven to see Jesus.

I asked permission from the funeral Director to go downstairs and view him. He was lying there with a sheet covering him, except for his face. I pulled the sheet back and saw the V shape across his chest as an autopsy had been conducted, and he had been embalmed.

Tears quietly rolling down my face, I questioned myself, *"Why didn't I just flip out?"*

What is wrong with my emotions? Was I numb? Sad? Shocked? Mad? Relieved? Content?

How dare he leave me? I was only 21! I knew only a life in a dictatorship and fear.

Who was going to give me purpose… in defilement?

From that point, again, I do not have much recollection of events other than a conflict between my father's sister Nejah, & most of the Arab community who insisted his wishes be carried out and be sent back home to Palestine for final burial.

What my Umptie did not realize was he had become a Christian and accepted Jesus Christ into his heart a couple of years prior; he was so ill with his heart before he went in for open heart surgery a couple of years beforehand. Mother told us that he was on the couch when Rev. Patrick (who is now passed) came by to visit as he sometimes did and told us of them watching the 700 Club together and that is when my father made his commitment to the Lord. However, he did not make this public to the Arab community. He was so powerful and so committed to the P.L.O (Palestinian Liberation Organization) that he did not want his new faith to interfere with all he was and had accomplished just yet. He was a child in his new walk of Christianity. There would be chaos, for sure. After his first heart surgery, he decided to fully retire from the grocery stores and spend half the year in Arizona. Ha! Come to find out that is where he began again to send uniforms for the P.L.O underground. Dad always had a means behind the madness. I can still remember his words.

"Yabba, never start anything unless you can see the end ".

The senator at the time (do the math), who was well connected with my father and a few of the Nickell brothers, was willing to step in and block my father being cargo shipped overseas. We were appalled that when being sent overseas like that, other than military, the casket would be opened at every port and checked for paraphernalia. It would take weeks for his arrival. However, the Israelis took care of that for us. They notified the American Council that they would not allow his body to come back to Israel, his country, *Palestine.*

Chapter Fourteen

BIG AL IS GONE

For days to come, it seemed my mother was forever putting out fires on behalf of my father. Mom was just 47 when he passed. She would become overwhelmed by protocol alone after a spouse passes, let alone dealing with his family, and even some of her own when it came to dad's finances. Ursula and I were busy hunting down the woman my father had his last affair with *Heather*. She worked at a local bar on Belmont Avenue in Liberty, Ohio, *The Boat House.*

The day came when it was time to pay Heather a visit; this would have turned out better for her had she not had an Arab man… and get this, he was the same man (Fiaz) who I was sent overseas within my younger years take her to visit my father in between visiting hours. My mother happened to be there, and Fiaz saw my mother and turned right back around. Shame on him for being so inconsiderate of my mother's feelings, let alone my father's respectability in the community. How would Fiaz even begin to explain who she was if asked!!!? What, A friend who did not know he passed and wanted to see him? Even I would not have believed that.

Just like the time Ursula and I went to see him in the hospital, this was after I had married Ralph, and my father did not have a contract out on me. So, we walked into the hospital room, said our hello's, and there we saw a beautiful vase of flowers with a card that said, *"Get well soon, Love H."*

Naturally, we asked him about it; it was screaming guilt and hilarity. My father was a spit'n and a sputer'n about *Harry*; the wholesaler produce guy downtown. Dad knew he was in trouble, my sister and I both looked at him, laughing, saying... *"Is that what we are going with?"* My father then asked us to go down the hall and get him some snacks, which we thought was strange, but we did as he asked and stepped out for a smoke as well. In hospitals, you could still smoke in designated areas; go figure. We returned to my father's room. Ha! The card was gone and never mentioned again. Shocker Shocker!! But after his death, we knew it was Heather who came to see him at the funeral home in-between visitation hours.

Mother confronted Fiaz about him bringing Heather to view my father; he did admit to it and said, *"She was so sad; I felt sorry for her."* All that tells me is my father must have had a long-term relationship with her long enough for his Arab, high-class friends/ cousins to be aware of it and know her. Once I heard about Heather coming to visit my father between visiting hours and having eye contact with my mother, it was time for me to go pay her a visit at the bar she worked in.

Ursula was out and about looking; however, Mary was with me on this day. A familiar officer/ security guard on duty, as I have thought about it over the years, Srg. Dewer was there for Heather's protection.

It was like Heather was aware she was in trouble with the family.

Immediately as we walked in, Dewer asked me not to come in. I told him he had no reason to deny me. I had my ID ready; he knew I was 21, especially since Mary had been dating him (even as a married man) for a while when she and I were roommates living on top of Whacky's Bar. Oh, yes, we would hop in police cars at night and go for rides with him and his partner; we always had a blast. I have a crazy story to tell you about Mary, Dewer & myself in another chapter.

Jack asked me to promise I would not start any trouble; I told him I would do my best not to cause a raucous. So, Mary and I are, I would say, 2 drinks in, and I just could not let it go.

Heather was a ridiculously cute gal with short, naturally curly blonde hair and big, gorgeous blue eyes, perhaps all of 25 years of age. Finally, as she was inside the bar on my side washing glasses, the time had come; this little girl was going down. I said hello to her, and she responded. I asked her where we had met before, and she looked extremely familiar. She could not recall.

So, I took that response as an opportunity to jog her memory a bit. I asked if she knew Al Salman; you would have thought she had seen a ghost. She replied, *"No, I don't think so. "*

I said, *"Well, let me introduce myself; I am Deana, his daughter. "Can you tell me for what reason you felt it proper to go pay your respects...while his wife was still at the funeral home?"* And there you have it; I yanked her by the front of the shirt, both hands and dragged her 98lb body right over the bar and started wailing on her. Dewer to the rescue, but slow enough to give me the time to do what I needed to do!! It was over as fast as it started.

Mary and I escorted out, Dewer saying, *"You Promised CJ."*

CJ (Camel Jockey) is the street name I carried for years in Youngstown and Toledo, Ohio. I just looked at Dewer and said, *"It was better to ask for forgiveness instead of permission in this case."* He winked at me, and I knew then that he knew it was going to happen; he let it happen and then came to be security and do his job. I felt vindicated for my mother. She did not deserve that type of disrespect as she was trying to bury her husband.

Tradition in the Islamic faith, *Khatam*: mourning for 40 days, then the *Spoua*: Prayer gathering after 7 days. Then comes a dinner, *Arbyin*, to honor the memory of the lost loved one after 40 days. The traditional food is called *Mansuf*. This is made with Lamb and or Chicken & rice in a savory yogurt sauce, then laid on top of Syrian flatbread. Sauce to overflow into the pan.

Given how big the gathering was, Mansuf was served on plates with flatware. When you are in someone's home as a guest of welcome, perhaps marriage, and even a passing, you use your hands to eat. Think about it...no one has ever used your hands to eat with, however, someone has usually eaten off most of the flatware.

You stay within your space, gather around the huge, round, what we call a Saneahh pan and use your hand to take bread, meat & rice into a ball ball, then dipped in the sauce and eat. It is actually a ridiculously awesome experience. I receive a bonding every time towards a true loving Arab long-established custom of consuming a family meal.

On the 40th day, my aunt Nejah showed up in street clothes. Whoa! Wait! What! Where was her thobe & hajjab?

Everyone in the Arab community did not seem to be shocked; the non-Americans did not know the difference. Come to find out, Nejah took her mourning back home to Palestine with her so she could be with other siblings and relatives, but more importantly, to clean out all my father's accounts since she had Power of Attorney. She had also returned to the United States before the 40 days in order to wrap up bank transactions that she had with my father, unbeknownst to my mother.

You see, the night before my father's surgery leading to his death, his 1st cousin, *Slaman*, was sitting by his bedside in the Cleveland Clinic Hospital hospital, in Cleveland, Ohio; this is where and when my father told *Slaman* that the minute he gets over this surgery and out of the hospital, he was going overseas and taking Nejah off of all the paperwork and taking back power of attorney. We never did understand my father's reasoning for this, and my mother never knew that this had even happened because she had no idea, he had left approximately 3 million dollars in Palestine.

As well off as they were financially in the United States, it was nothing compared to overseas. The war began, and attorneys hired, even a Jewish attorney, to include flying overseas and filing in the courts. The Arab family court was completely different than other courts. They sided with the *Muslim* side of the family. Mother went to the extent of having a paper stating that my sister Ursula and I were of Muslim faith, which really surprised us both. It was rejected.

My mother would not sign off that she was a Muslim; she, too, gave her heart to Jesus on April 1st, 1971. As most of us, it takes years to really understand and come to KNOW the Lord. I, for one, am still learning forgiveness. But I guess she figured it was ok to do that on behalf of her children…or was it? Humm? Nothing ever became of it other than dead ends. In later years I returned to Palestine to collect what we eventually found out was left as stocks in a cigarette company in Jerusalem, and the Arab courts had no control over that money. I will tell you how my sister Ursula and I were able to get the money out of Palestine into the country Jordan in the next series.

THE BURIAL DAY

The day of burial arrived. The sky was full of gray clouds only to open and downpour. People from all over the United States, Palestine & Jordan came. It was overwhelming. The cemetery was not far, less than a mile. The procession began. There were so many cars that the line went from the cemetery all the way back to the funeral home. His people were walking in the street out of respect; never mind, there would not have been room for cars regardless.

The burial was complete. My father was laid to rest. I have no remembrance other than the rain, umbrellas, hearing wailing from the Arab women, chanting/prayers from the Arab men. The rest, silently praying, realizing a legend of short term is gone. Afterwards everyone was invited to the *"Nadi,* "the Arab Club, for food. The Nadi was bursting at the seams; once people got their food and sat at the long tables to eat, they quickly moved and gave their seats up, stood or went outside (especially the smokers…everyone, except the women). It was there where I ran into my ex-father-in-law!! Miscal's father, Suliman.

His eyes were piercing! Clearly, he wished I were in that casket. I met his eyes only to reciprocate the same thoughts! Our family cousin and friend Nasser was there and knew what was about to happen; he gently came over to me and guided me out of Suliman's sight. I will never forget the look in Nasser's eyes. Sadness & Love. A legend…Forever Gone…His legacy living on!!!

As you continue to journey with me, you will read more

Tragic Whispers!!!

Fateeh Abdel Fatah Salman (Big Al)

(Dar Toweel) * The Big House

May 21st, 1929-April 12th, 1983

"Airquad Fi Salam "

Rest In Peace

Inna IiIlahi Wa Inna Ilayhi Raji'un

Indeed, we belong to God, and indeed, to Him, we will return.

Holy Land Prayer

And the dust returns to the earth as it was, and the spirit returns to God who gave it.

Ecclesiastes 12:7

Amen

To Be Continued